TEMPERED BY FIRE

THE TRUE STORY OF
PHYLLIS BARKER DILLEY BACKHAUS

By Phyllis Backhaus

Bear Paw Publishing
Houston, Alaska

Copyright: Phyllis Backhaus ©
All rights reserved

Photographs from the collection of Phyllis Backhaus
and by Dr. Robert Mallin, M.D.

Cover Photograph from the collection of Phyllis Backhaus
Cover Insert Photograph by Dr. Robert Mallin, M.D.

First Printing, December 1998

Published by: Bear Paw Publishing
             Wonderland Drive
             PO Box 940024
             Houston, Alaska
             (907) 892-6638

Library of Congress Catalog Card Number:
98-073875
ISBN 9-9661665-1-5

For Additional Copies Contact:
       Bear Paw Publishing
       PO Box 940024
       Houston, Alaska 99694
To order individual copies of "Tempered by Fire" mail check or money order for $19.95 plus $3.00 book rate shipping and handling to the above noted address.

Discounts are available for booksellers. Call 907-892-6638 for more information.

Dedication

This book is dedicated to the memory of my first husband, Dave Dilley and to our children and their spouses, Glenn and Suzie Dilley, Cindy and Mark Riley and Rick and Paige Dilley and to our grandchildren, Brittany, Caalee and Laurel Dilley, Metis and Chelsey Riley and Aryel and David Dilley. I also dedicate this book to my beloved husband, Russell Backhaus and his daughters, Tammy Klein and Shaye Floden and his grandchildren, Courtney (Corky) and Cassidy Klein and Shaun Mathis.

What treasures from God you all are!

Introduction

This is a true story about life, love, honor, tragedy, faith and the help of God and His angels. This book was written at the urging and encouragement of my family and friends. I am using this opportunity to thank those whom I never properly thanked during my rescue and recovery from the plane crash that took my husband, Dave Dilley, and left me severely burned:

The Air Force rescue crew that responded from Elmendorf Air Force Base, near Anchorage, Alaska to the crash site near Petersville, Alaska. I never did learn your names, but I thank you from the bottom of my heart.

The doctors, nurses, therapists and the other wonderful employees at Providence Hospital, Anchorage, Alaska, who took such good care of me. I could not fully appreciate everything you did for me then, because at the time I could not know that all the things you did to me were for my own good and healing.

My husband Dave's sister and brother-in-law, Betty and Loren Dodds.

My boss at Dimond High School, Anchorage, Eva Reese, who came to see me every single day in the hospital for a solid three months. I know that God will bless you for your caring and I want you to know that I waited every day to hear the familiar steps clicking in the hall at 3:00 p.m. For most of that time, I was not a pretty sight, and I appreciate your not letting that stop your caring.

I appreciate my Mom and Dad, whom I know are in heaven, for all the blessings of life you gave me and for showing me the faith I needed to carry on through trials.

I also appreciate all my friends and neighbors for their faithful help to my family in our desperate time of need and who lent their support in so many ways to my three teen-age children who had to become adults in such a tragic situation.

Finally, but not least, God bless all those who I've had the opportunity to touch in times of tragedy and hopelessness and was able to help because of what I went through.

I hope that you, the reader of this book, will find strength also.

I want you to understand my background so that you can better understand my story. I was born in Spearfish, South Dakota, which is the home of the Passion Play and the gateway to the beautiful Black Hills. Rock formations known as "rim rocks" are common in that area.
I have one older brother, Charles (who I call "Chuck"). My father worked at the power plant on Redwater Creek, between Spearfish and Belle Fouche.

I grew up in what I consider to be a perfect setting. All of my friends and the neighbor kids thought I lived in the White House because there was a flagpole with a billowing American flag right by my upstairs bedroom window. The whole place was meticulously kept--manicured lawn, blooming flower garden, always looking freshly painted.

My Mom was beautiful and tiny at 4'11" in her high heels. (Dad called her "Tiny"). Our home was filled with love and kindness, faith in the Lord and compassion for all. All the kids were always welcome and the cookie jar was always full.

I was considered physically beautiful and won beauty pageants and at one time was a contender for Miss South Dakota.

This is my story. Hopefully it will touch others and help them to accept life after disfigurement and other tragedies that may scar them for life.

Just remember that God will not give us more than we, with His help, can bear. What He gives us is a test to make us stronger.

My brother and me (on the right) 'helping' on Grandpa's farm

Chapter 1

When we are going through life, we don't know what will happen along the way. Although we can't predict what will come our way, or how we will react to it, I believe that we are shaped by our families and our faith. I have been fortunate to be blessed with strong family and strong faith. Both have been constant for me throughout the ups and downs of life.

My Dad operated the power plant on Redwater Creek between Belle Fouche and Spearfish, South Dakota. We lived close to my Grandpa and Grandma Bryan, who lived on a farm, and we liked to spend time at their place in the summer helping with the heavy work of the season. Well, actually Chuck was a lot of help, but I don't know how much help I was the summer I was twelve, which is where this story begins. I do know that I always had fun at my grandparents' home with all the animals and the chores to do.

Chuck left all the critters to me, which I especially enjoyed. Horses seem to share a bond with me and I could ride many that other people couldn't ride. I wasn't (and still am not) big enough to make them do anything, but they seem to trust me. One advantage of being small was that Grandpa let me ride some horses that weren't really ready to be ridden by anyone very big.

I have a special place in my heart for animals and the outdoors. In many scenes in my memory, I see warm, muggy evenings, twinkling, pulsing stars, the dust and exhaustion of a long day riding horses, cows satisfied from having been drained of their milk and with a full stomach, and chickens in bed. I also see laughing neighbors around a kitchen table playing cards in the evening while the neighbor children, my brother and I played outside in the increasing darkness. Catching fireflies in pint jars from Grandma's cellar were a part of the picture. My memories of going through reeds and cattails to the pond to catch whatever creatures we could find and to listen to the frogs, the crickets and the baby blackbirds all singing with the surge of new life all come back as I reflect on my childhood.

I remember the smells and the sounds of leading the smaller children through the meadow and watching the lights of the fireflies and taking the jar and very carefully getting into position to slip the flying light into captivity with great gentleness. When I had gathered enough single little lights, I had a lantern to help light the way home. It was especially fun when little kids who had never seen this miracle before join our evening adventures. We always made a point to take the fireflies back to where we found them after disrupting the game of the grownups to show off our treasures.

After what seemed like too short a time, the neighbors would signal with their car horn that it was time to leave, which meant that it was also time for my brother and me to go to the house and get ready for bed. I liked to go to Chuck's room to watch him build model airplanes and visit a bit before we had to say goodnight. Chuck is the best brother that anyone could have had. We didn't fight like most brothers and sisters, and sometimes he even let me help with his model airplanes! Most nights we practiced our Hawaiian steel guitars thirty minutes like our Mom expected us to do, but sometimes we were just too tired from a full day of being children in the country to comply with her instructions. We were usually pretty good about doing what we were told, but we were children! Because we liked to play our guitars and I sang at community affairs, we usually practiced until Grandma stuck her head in the door and told us it was time to go to bed.

So, after a quick bath and a fast prayer, I would slip into the comfort of clean, crisp, wind-dried sheets, which still held the fragrance of South Dakota in the summer. I would fluff my pillow, squirm just right and fall to sleep.

One night during the summer I was twelve, I had either a nightmare, or a vision. Only God knows which, but I know that I woke up, heart racing and sitting up in my bed. A man's hand was on my arm. He didn't say a word, but I knew it was a man, but he didn't have a head! I had also seen beautiful golden stairs over a shimmering creek. After awhile, my heart stopped racing and I fell asleep again. I slept the rest of the night until it was time to get up and have another busy day. I was anxious to see my Dad who was coming over to help work on building the garage. He was a perfectionist in his work and could do everything. Mom would come with him to do the laundry and to clean Grandma's house, so I knew that I would be made to do the dusting--she didn't seem to understand that I had better things to do (like catching frogs)--than dust!

About 7:00 a.m. the phone rang and Dad told us that they wouldn't be over because they had to go to Sundance, Wyoming, where his parents lived.

Although my Dad hadn't said a word about anything being wrong, I started to cry and sob with a broken heart and told my Grandma that my Grandpa Barker was dead and I knew because he came in the night to tell me. Grandma turned white and had to sit down while she tried to comfort me while I sat on her lap.

Grandpa and Chuck were bringing the milk in from the separator shed and Grandma called them in and told them that Dad would call back in two hours. All Grandma knew at this point was that my Dad had to go help Grandma Barker. Both my grandparents tried to calm me down, but I kept insisting that Grandpa Barker was dead.

After awhile, they tried to go on with the activities of the day and I went to my bedroom to get dressed to go to the corral. I had to talk to God about this and I could talk to Him while I was with the horses. Once in awhile one of the horses nuzzled me with a velvety soft nose and seemed to understand my terrible sadness.

The barn cats came and rubbed against my legs and arched their backs in sympathy, too. I sat down on a feed bucket and asked God to make this a real nightmare and that it not be true. "Please God, please God, don't take my Grandpa away" I prayed over and over.

A little later, Grandpa Bryan came into the corral and put his arms around me in a big, protective hug. Then he told me that Grandpa Barker's truck brakes had gone out on a steep hill. His helper had jumped out and Grandpa thought he could ride it out. His driveline had broken and he couldn't even shift to a lower gear. The truck ran off the last curve and had rolled over. Grandpa's neck was broken and he had died in the accident.

That was the first tragedy in my first twelve years. I had lived a happy, secure and absolutely glorious life. I had been raised with the knowledge and faith that every living thing has to die, so that they can have everlasting life. Grandpa Bryan took me to the alfalfa field where the first cutting of hay lay in neat, sweet-smelling stacks and asked me if I remembered in the fall how the hay had quit growing and seemed to be dead. But, in the spring, it had come back to life. He reminded me that we all die, too, but spring back to life in heaven, that our soul is never dead, but will come back in a beautiful, fresh body.

My heart was still broken for a long, long time, but I finally got on with my life. I stayed with Grandma Barker a lot. We both missed my Grandpa Barker so much.

We had to go through his things and Grandma had decided to sell Grandpa Barker's pickup, so we were taking everything out of it. I opened the glove box and found a new pack of Black Jack gum. That really tore my heart out because Grandpa always had his Black Jack gum and I missed him all the more. But, after that day, it seemed that I healed from my grief

Chapter 2

I always loved school. I was in all the plays, the band and glee club and had friends of all ages. I enjoyed going to school and being with my friends and enjoyed the teachers and even the lessons!

All my classes went along well and the happiness of home and family stayed the same with little variation.

Then came the winter of 1949 when I was thirteen.

One morning it was snowing really hard so Dad took us to the bus stop. All the kids, being kids, were excited about the heavy snow and we set about planning for a fun weekend of skiing, sledding, and hot dog roasts. We could even hook a toboggan behind a horse. When we tied the toboggan to the saddle horn with a rope. Then, we would go for miles along the country roads listening to the silence and only occasionally hearing the noise of the creaking of saddle leather, the squeak of hooves on snow, the huffing of the horse and our own laughter. If we decided to have the horse run, we had fun ducking the snowballs that his flying feet threw at us.

We often had fun-filled weekends with our friends but were ready to go back to school on Monday to share our adventures and to hear what our other friends had done over the weekend, so we thought this might be another opportunity for that kind of fun.

During the first class on that particular Monday, the wind came up and started blowing the snow around and all we could see was white. We lived in the foothills of the Black Hills, so there wasn't a lot to block the path of the wind. We knew from experience that, if the wind continued to blow the way it was, that our way home would be blocked, so we were ready when the Principal came and told us the buses were coming back to take us home immediately. The drifts were already getting so deep that the bus could hardly make it through.

Then, about three miles from our house, the driver got stuck in a big drift. We were as close as we were going to get to our homes. One of our neighbors, Mr. Jeffreys, was there with his team of horses and sled to take my brother and me and his son, Jerry, the rest of the way home. Mr. Jeffreys knew that the bus probably wouldn't make it all the way through, in that kind of weather, so he had set out to go as far as he needed to until he met the bus.

Mr. Jeffreys had lots of blankets in the sled for us to snuggle in and a big pile of hay to sit on, on the floor of the sled

I still don't know how the horses could see anything or how they knew the way home, but they did so off we went. It was scary and fun at the same time.

The horses had a hard job and were huffing and puffing and were lathered with sweat. Their nostrils were flared with the effort. They had to lunge through the drifts, which were getting bigger and deeper all the time as the wind continued to blast. It wasn't long before the horses were caked in ice from the sweat, which had frozen on their strong, beautiful bodies.

It took two hours of this effort to reach Mr. Jeffreys' house. When we got there, Mr. Jeffreys got as close to the porch as he could, then he took a length of rope out of the sled and after tying one end to the sled, he struggled to find the porch where he tied the other end to the porch railing. After he gave us the signal that it was tied, Chuck, Jerry and I made our way along the rope to the porch. We hung on for dear life as we trudged, floundered and fell before we finally got there safely. Then, Mr. Jeffreys went back along the rope to the sled. He had lots of extra rope in the sled, for just this type of situation. He tied enough rope to reach the barn to the end that had been tied to the sled and then let it play along the snow as the horses made their way back to the barn. He let them lead the way, as their sense of direction in the blizzard was better than his. When they got to the barn, the horses went straight into the wagon bay, pulling the sled with them. Mr. Jeffreys then tied the end of the rope to a secure spot in the barn.

He was gone a long time, feeding, watering, brushing down and putting their blankets on them. Mr. Jeffreys knew that without his horses, we wouldn't have been safe and he was thanking them by taking such good care of them.

As soon as he was done tending to the horses, he made his own way back along the rope life line to the warmth and welcome of his own family and my brother and me in the snug and fragrant kitchen of the farmhouse. We treated him like the hero he was for saving us from the storm.

As you can imagine, Mom and Dad were frantic. Their car was drifted into the garage and they couldn't go anywhere. But, the phone lines were still up. They hadn't heard anything about how Chuck and I were, other than Mrs. Jeffreys had called them when her husband took the team of horses and sled to meet the bus. But, that was hours before and they had no idea if Mr. Jeffreys had made it, if the bus had made it to where he was or if we had even made it back to the Jeffreys home. They could pray for our safety but could do nothing else. As soon as Mrs. Jeffreys knew that we were safe at her home, she called our parents and told them that we would spend the night, as it was far too dangerous to try to go any further. Besides, the horses were exhausted.

Of course, Chuck and I didn't mind a bit. We were good friends with the Jeffreys family and we knew we would have a fun time being snow bound. We played monopoly and canasta and drank hot cocoa. We told stories, and Mr. Jeffreys reminded me of the time that I was on one of my many nature walks and found a little skunk which was all alone, and I thought deserted. I had picked him up and he hadn't even tried to bite me. I thought he was so cute. I took the skunk with me to the power plant, where my Dad stood in the doorway. He saw me coming and warned me to take the skunk back across the bridge and turn him loose. Like the obedient daughter I usually was, I did as he asked and it was a good thing, because" he was already more than a little upset with me! He said I smelled worse than the skunk! My friend, Nancy came along and we decided to go horseback riding. (Incidentally, Nancy never told me I smelled like a skunk!)

On our ride, we saw Grandpa Jeffreys (Mr. Jeffreys' father) irrigating the sugar beets, so we rode over to say "Hi" and to visit a little. I was still insulted that my Dad had said I smelled like a skunk and I told Grandpa Jeffreys that my Dad thought I stunk like a skunk. Grandpa Jeffreys said, with a straight face, that he didn't know why my Dad would say such a thing! Later, all the neighbors got a good laugh about it because Grandpa Jeffreys said I did smell just like a skunk!

We had another good laugh about it that night and, after telling more stories, Mrs. Jeffreys sent us off to bed in one of her warm featherbed.

When we got up the next morning, it was clear, calm and cold. All the fences were buried. The snow was so packed from the wind-driven drifts, and the massive amount of snow, that the cows (and we) would walk anywhere on top of the snow. We walked the miles home across the fields, sliding down steep snowdrifts along the way. It would be a week before the roads were open.

Mom and Dad were happy to see us and all was well.

We continued to play in the snow after we got home. We dug a tunnel from the house to the garage and played in it for about a week until Dad told us the sun beating on the snow was making our tunnel weak and he was afraid it would cave in on us. So, we turned it into a deep canyon instead of a tunnel. We rode scoop shovels and a piece of old linoleum down the steep slope of the rim rock. Talk about a wild ride! We talked about taking an old car hood from the dump and riding on it, but weren't ambitious enough to dig it out.

The storm, which we children enjoyed so much, was a real tragedy to our farm and ranch neighbors. Many animals died, most of which suffocated during the first of the storm when the snow was drifting. It was very bad and it took a long time to find all the animals and to assess the damage.

In a few weeks, though, our life was back to normal--school, amateur shows, playing and singing with our cousin Boyd. We even had costumes and every time we sang at a function in the community we had to sing "Dearie"! We entertained many times and enjoyed every minute of it.

As always, life went on and summer came again. That summer was really busy. Chuck worked for Grandpa, helping with the farming. I helped out by milking cows. I remember that there's nothing like getting swatted in the face with a not-too-clean tail full of cockleburs! I loved all the farm chores and seeing to it that the barn cats got their squirts of milk, which they had earned by catching mice.

Chapter 3

Of course, I still had a soft spot of any kind of animal and thought that the pink little baby pigs were the cutest things in this marvelous world! There was one in Grandpa's litter, which was a runt, and I mean a RUNT. He was starving, so I got to keep him in a box in my bedroom. I named him "Bo Jo" and took tender, loving, care of him. He eventually got healthy and soon was a real nuisance. Then I had to make a pen for him outside, close to the other pigs. He followed me everywhere, just like a puppy. We would go to the stock pond and the swamp and he even followed me when I took lunch to the fields for Grandpa and Chuck. By the time summer was over and it was time to go back to school, Bo Jo was big and strong and could live with the other pigs.

One day on my nature adventures, I came across a big bull snake in the nest of a cottontail rabbit. He already had two big lumps in his body and was in the process of swallowing a third baby rabbit. There were three more babies in the nest, so I scooped them up and went straight home. For two weeks, I fed them warm milk. Since I didn't have a tiny baby bottle, I soaked cotton balls in warm milk. Then, after the first few sucks, the babies made their own nipple from the cotton. They grew up just fine. When they got big enough to go outside, they hung around the yard for awhile. I was afraid my cat or dog would bother them, but they never did. The rabbits finally did go back to the wild.

One hot summer day, I was playing horse. I had canned milk cans stomped on my feet for hooves (this was really good for my shoes, you know!). I tied a scarf on the backside of my coveralls for my tail. When I ran around, the cans made me sound like a real horse.

I was crossing the creek in a shallow spot, jumping from rock to rock, so I wouldn't get wet. But, my "hooves" were wet and slick, and you can guess that I slipped on a rock! After lots of windmilling with my arms and some fancy footwork, I finally fell into the water.

As I stood up, dripping wet and floundering, I heard a rustle in the weeds on the other side of the creek. I figured it was probably a muskrat. But, being the critter person that I am, I had to check it out, so I waded over to see what was there. There were two baby raccoons. They were skinny and weak and could hardly walk. Of course, I came to the rescue and picked them up, cradled in my arms. I splashed back across the creek and hustled home.

I kept the raccoons in a box by my bed. I lined the box with one of my Mom's precious new rugs. I fed them milk and canned dog food. There was a boy and a girl. I named the boy "Randy" and he got to be a real pest. But the girl never got very friendly. After they got bigger, they stayed outside and were free to come and go. Randy stayed around our place for a long time.

You know, raccoons wash everything they eat. Randy loved ginger snap cookies. He would take them to his big water pan where he washed everything. His little hands were really busy, and then he would get this funny look on his face and desperately feel for his cookie, which had dissolved!

If Randy got in the house, he would trundle up the steps to the cupboard and throw everything off. He would watch, intrigued, until objects quit moving, then would throw something else off. This went on until the shelf was cleared off. Of course, the floor wasn't too tidy by then! After about a year, Randy left for good.

Randy the raccoon, Sparky the dog and Snowball the rabbit

I also had a chipmunk. I had beautiful new Priscilla curtains in my bedroom. One day, we were going to Sundance, and I didn't want my chipmunk to have to breathe stale air, so I made sure that my window was open and put the cage in the window. Of course, the chipmunk saw my beautiful curtains as good material for a nest, so he chewed those curtains to bits and worked them into his cage. I can tell you that my meticulous Mom didn't appreciate that at all, even though the chipmunk had a wonderful new nest!

Over the years, my collection of pets included a bat and several mice. I used to take the mice for rides in the livestock car on Chuck's electric train. One day, my friend Nancy was helping me play with the mice and was taking them out of the train when one bit her. She, of course, threw it in the air to get it off her, and it got loose in the playroom. I didn't tell Mom or Dad that I had a mouse on the loose in the playroom, because I was afraid they would have set a trap for it.

Several months later, Mom was getting a quilt out of the linen closet and found that a mouse had chewed on five of her beautiful, handmade quilts. I'm not sure if Mom figured out that one of my pets was the culprit, or if she thought a wild one had come in and done the damage.

The pet, which proved to be the scariest, in hindsight, was the snake I had. My Uncle Morris (Mom's brother) found a snake in the lumber which was stockpiled for a new bridge which was being built on the country road over Spearfish Creek, and he brought it home. He, of course, knew that I adopted any, and all, critters that came my way, and he was not disappointed.

I took the snake and named him "Rainbow" and carried him around in the pocket of my leather jacket. We didn't know what kind of snake it was, but figured it was one of the harmless ones, which were common in our area. He got his name from the wide bands of red, black and yellow bands along his body.

One day, I was visiting my Dad at the power plant, and a man from the head office was there. I had to show Rainbow to him. When I got Rainbow out of my pocket, the man turned pale and I thought he was going to faint. He asked Dad if he knew what kind of snake it was, and he said "No". The man told him was a coral snake, but Dad told him there were no coral snakes in South Dakota. The man insisted that was what it was and suggested that it had come in on the load of lumber for the bridge.

Dad decided right then and there that we had to take the snake to the Reptile Gardens in Rapid City, South Dakota, the first thing the next morning. In the meantime, I had to keep Rainbow in his box. When we got to the reptile garden, we found out for sure that my friend was a deadly coral snake. I learned that just one bite from that snake would have killed me instantly. Dad couldn't figure out why I hadn't been bitten, and we were told that it takes a lot to get a coral snake agitated and they don't bite unless they get hurt or agitated. I sure was thankful that I hadn't pinched him while I was handling him! We were used to rattlesnakes, which have fangs, but we found out that coral snakes just chew on you. Needless to say, the Reptile Gardens gained a new tenant that day!

Chapter 4

As we got older, Dad put a motor on a bicycle and bought a Cushman scooter so Chuck and I both had wheels. We sure had a lot of fun and it kept me on the road. One time, Chuck and the neighbor boy were trying to hide from us girls. We had the scooter. In the process of trying to hide from us, Chuck and his friend turned off their light and proceeded to drive right through the barbed wire gate. (They didn't know that someone had closed the gate, which was usually left open.) We heard all the commotion as we rode by, but just thought that they were trying to scare us. Later, two beat up boys showed up at the house. It took Mom more than a few bandages to patch them up.

Chuck had always built model airplanes with motors, which were really nice. One day, we were playing with his model airplanes and the grass was too high for a regular take-off, so he had me run with the plane. It came around so fast that I couldn't dive away quickly enough and the plane hit me in the behind and broke the prop on the plane. My brother wasn't a bit worried about me, but he had to check his plane over good for other damage.

On Saturdays, we went to town for groceries, and after the shopping was done, we would meet the neighbor kids for fun trips to the roller rink or to the movies. Our favorite movie was "Black Arrow", a short movie before the feature.

We played Black Arrow a lot, and used neckties for our headbands as we ran around the rim rock. At the time, we never considered what kind of condition those ties, which we remembered to return to the tie rack, were in! You can imagine that our sweaty, dirty, play didn't leave them in a condition our Dads would want to wear with their dress clothes. Usually they were in their work clothes, and only dressed up, to the point of wearing a tie, for funeral. I wonder now if they ever figured out what happened to their ties!

My mother's sister, Aunt Lucille, and her husband, Uncle Bill, had a ranch by Crow Peak. They had a daughter, who I called "Mary C", and a son, Billy. I liked to stay there and ride their horses. I was several years older than they were, so I taught the kids how to ride. My Dad had never liked horses because one of his friends had been dragged to death when he fell off and got his foot tangled in the stirrup, so I could have anything but a horse. But, I asked Uncle Bill if I could keep a horse at his place, and he agreed. So, the first chance we got, we went to the horse sale and when they brought in a dapple-gray Arabian, I had to have him. Uncle Bill got him for me for $40.00. He wasn't broken to ride, but that didn't' bother me any. I trained him and no one else could ride him. I finally had a horse that was strictly mine! He was so handsome. I kept him brushed to a glossy shine all the time. He never needed shoes and could run forever across the grassy plain.

There's nothing like the exhilaration of racing in the wind, hair flying, riding bareback with the strong rhythm of the muscles of the horse moving you along. My cousin Mary C was really afraid to ride, but when she had had an out-of-control horse run away with her, and she was able to stay on a it (bareback, no less she became more confident.

In fact, Billy and I hadn't even done anything to help her with the runaway—we just sat on the hill and watched the horse in flight. After that, we all had a lot of fun with our horses.

We had to help Uncle Bill milk sometimes, or I would help Aunt Lucille in the garden. We had our own candy drawer, which was always kept full. Aunt Lucille was the best cook and always served lots of delicious food.

Riding my Grandpa's horse   Dressed for entertaining

Chapter 5

Whenever I got a chance in the summertime, I went to stay with Aunt Marie and Uncle Leonard at their ranch at Martin, South Dakota. Aunt Marie was a schoolteacher and Uncle Leonard took care of the ranch. He was also a pilot, and during World War II he was a flight instructor for the Air Force. He had been stationed in Texas and when they moved back to South Dakota, he still occasionally taught people how to fly.

When I was 14, and Chuck 16, he taught us how to fly. It was a wonderful experience. I thoroughly enjoyed the experience of watching the deer, fox, coyote and other wildlife as we glided over the Sand Hills and Badlands of South Dakota and northwestern Nebraska.

It didn't' take either Chuck or me very long to become pretty good at flying a plane. When Chuck did his first solo flight, he was like a pro. Then it was my turn. I was a nervous wreck. I knew just what to do and when to do it, but I was still scared.

Uncle Leonard finally lost his patience with me and told me to get into the plane and do exactly what I had been taught to do. So, I started out. I revved the engine and taxied to the end of the runway, all the way to the end! I spun the plane around and headed back down the runway. Then, when my speed was just right, I maneuvered the flaps into the proper position and up I went!

It was wonderful! I made a big circle over the glistening dunes, and then I got worried about how I would land. I'd done the landing by myself many times, but Uncle Leonard had been with me. This was different, even though the steps were the same.

I brought the plane down, even with the runway, and almost on the ground. Then panic took over. I took the plane back up. I had to be sure that I was clear of the phone line before I landed.

The longer I stayed up, the more scared I got. Uncle Leonard was losing patience with me. He had already taken his hat off and thrown it on the ground. He was waving his arms at me and I could see his mouth moving, so I knew he that he was telling me to land! I knew that I didn't have a lot of gas, and that I would have to land soon.

By then, Uncle Leonard was stomping up and down on his hat and it had become a ragged mess. Although I couldn't hear his words, I could imagine that they weren't too clean!

After four "touch and go's", I finally had no choice but to land. So, I brought the plane down for the final descent, lined it up with the runway, and finally just dropped in! It was a real jolt. The propeller broke when I hit the ground and the left landing gear was a little bent. That was all the damage I did, but Uncle Leonard was still very upset with me. In fact, he stormed around declaring that I was the last female that he ever intended to try to teach to fly!

I'm sure that Chuck was enjoying every minute of the display. I was just happy to be walking around in one piece. Chuck still flies, but that was my first and last solo flight. Uncle Leonard had started a crop dusting business, which takes real skill. He kept flying and farming right up to the time of his death.

Chapter 6

Once, Chuck and his friend, Walt, decided to build a wind machine. He had a frame from a real airplane and put an airplane motor on the back with the propeller. We passengers lost more than one hat, as the wind blew them off into the propeller. He and his friends rode it down our country roads. It was a lot like the airboats we see today except it had wheels. When you stop to think about it, it was a dangerous machine considering it didn't even have a guard around the propeller. But, all the neighbors approved their children riding on it, and by the grace of God no one ever got hurt.

Another time, Dad and Chuck built a boat in the basement. It was sleek and beautiful. But, they forgot that they had to get it up the steps. So, they ended up having to take it apart to get it outside. It was almost a catastrophe, but they were successful and we enjoyed the boat for many years.

We did have our chores to do around the house, and we would try to do them as fast as we could so that we could go and play. I remember one time that I had to dust the steps three times before Mom would accept the job. It had to be perfect, and in my rush to play, I tried to get by and ended up taking more time than if I had done it right the first time. I finally learned to do a good job at whatever I did, thanks to my mother's insistence on doing the job right, no matter what it was.

When I was a freshman in high school, Dad quit working at the power plant and went to work for Lamperts Lumber, in Belle Fouche. They bought a new house and Mom worked as a waitress at the Don Pratt Hotel and Grill. I also worked there after school until 8:00 p.m., as a waitress, if I didn't have a school activity or practice.

We had the best childhood anyone could have. I know that both my parents have earned their reward in heaven for putting up with my brother (and me). To this day, I have a house full of critters, which no one else seems to want. I take in old dogs and hurt animals and find homes for them or patch them up. People are welcome too, and my grandchildren love to play, or stay, at my house. I guess that I can pass along some of the love I knew when I was growing up by taking in animals, kids and people and helping them along.

Riding my Cushman scooter in a school play with Dave Kruger

Chapter 5

As always, at the end of summer, I was anxious for school to start, but knew I would miss all the critters that had to stay on the farm.

The school year started and I got involved with activities again. Soon it was October and fall was in the air. The leaves were rustling in the trees and were turning bright colors of gold, red, and orange and some brown. Some were already fluttering to settle in the browning grass.

I had been selected to be a Page in the coronation for the new homecoming king and queen at Black Hills Teachers College. I was only thirteen and I was thrilled at the honor. This was a big event. The college football team, the Yellow Jackets, was playing for the State Championship that year (they did win). All the people from the surrounding area were in town for the festivities

After the game, my friends and I were to meet my brother, Chuck, for a ride home. They all had a crush on my brother and I thought they were silly. We saw him across the field, so took off across the fields to meet him, giggling all the way.

We got to where he was and found that he was talking to a strange guy who was tall, with light brown hair, blue eyes and big, strong shoulders. My heart skipped a beat when I saw him and I felt like I was melting on the spot! Chuck introduced us to Dave Dilley. We learned that he was new to the area and lived on a farm by Crow Peak. He had an older sister, Betty, and their family had just moved from Nemo, South Dakota.

Since Mom's sister, my Aunt Lucille, and her family had a ranch by Crow Peak, I decided on the spot that I had to find out more about this guy, Dave. I figured my aunt would be a good source of information.

It wasn't long before Dave started coming to see my brother, going fishing and doing all the things that boys do. Every time he came, my heart would do flip flops, but all my friends and I could do was ride the horses and primp a little. Before long, it was me that Dave was coming to see, instead of my brother, even though I was still only thirteen and wasn't allowed to have a "real" date until I was fifteen.

The Barker family, Mom and Dad, Chuck and me

When I would go to see Aunt Lucille, I would hope that Dave would ride his horse over and he often did. We had some wonderful times riding up Sand Creek or up in the hills. This place in the Black Hills was beautiful and so lush!

We both had good horses and I always rode bare back. The riding in the hills and along the creek were our best times! As time went on, we would occasionally go to a movie or go roller-skating with friends. Eventually, we started going to the dances every Saturday night with our parents, and the older ranchers and farmers. We danced with people of all ages and had an absolute ball square dancing, doing the "flying Dutchmen" or slow dancing.

As we spent more and more time together, we learned that we were really a pair of soul mates.

I wanted to take Dave to my high school prom, but the rule in our school (Belle Fouche High School) was that only students from our own high school could go. Since Dave went to Spearfish High School, I had to go with someone else, if I went, and I wasn't going to stay home! So, while I went to the prom with another boy, Dave waited for me at my house. That was hard for him to do! Fortunately, he was never the jealous type.

It turned out that I was the Queen of Hearts, and Bobby Gilbert, who was a dear friend and a "little person", who wouldn't grow anymore, was the King of Hearts. We were selected by the vote of the entire school, and it was a big honor.

By graduation time, Dave and I were madly in love. We both loved the same things and did fun things together. We couldn't wait until the weekends to see each other, so we decided to get married.

Dave Dilley's high school graduation picture

Phyllis Barker all dressed up for the high school prom

The local pageant leader, based on grades, personality, popularity and talent had selected me to represent our area in the Miss South Dakota pageant.

Mom and Dad were disappointed that I wanted to get married at that time as they wanted me to finish the run for "Miss South Dakota", then, they wanted me to go to college and further my music. My brother had enlisted in the Air Force by this time. But, they did love Dave so they gave us their blessings.

We had a simple church wedding and all our family and friends came to wish us well in our new life together.

Even though we were young, we knew that our love was special and would take us through thick and thin together.

We enjoyed the company of each other and found great joy in the every day things we had already done together, which would become even more special when we were truly working together as a team of husband and wife.

We had high hopes for the future and we had confidence in the abilities of each other to give strength and support to the other throughout our lifetime together.

Like all young couples, we didn't know all the adjustments which we would have to make to become one instead of two, but we were willing to do our best.

Our parents were in support of us, but they let us know that we were to look to each other instead of to them in times of working things out between us.

We were ready and eager to meet the challenges that were to come.

Dave and I wanted a home, not just a house. We looked forward to establishing our family and wanted to have children in due time.

We were ready for what we assumed would be our long life together.

Dave and Phyllis Dilley

Chapter 6

Dave was working on a ranch for Sid Nicholas, a bachelor friend of ours, and I was very welcome there. Our honeymoon was short and sweet--we just drove through the beautiful Black Hills for three days, and visited Mount Rushmore.

My first morning as a wife and cook turned out to be a disaster! Even though I had often fixed breakfast for my Dad and brother after my mother went to work in town, that morning I forgot the baking powder in the pancakes! The guys thought it was funny, but the dog and birds wouldn't even eat them!

Then, the first time I did the laundry also turned out to be a real catastrophe--everyone had the old-style wringer washers. I knew how to sort the clothes, so I did the whites first, with a little bleach, then the towels. The jeans and socks were really dirty, so by the time I threw them in, I decided I needed to add some more bleach, which I did, right on them! This was before the days when tie-dyed was in style. The only thing that those clothes were good for was rags--but they were clean! It didn't take me long to learn the right time and the right amount of bleach to add to the laundry, though.

They threw an old-fashioned shivaree for us, which was a big party where all the neighbors came late at night, clanging bells and making all kinds of noise. They brought food and little gifts. They also would sneak crumbs of cake and rice in the couple's bed. Anyway, everyone had a ball and we were good sports about it. After all, we had done it to other newlywed couples and would do it again.

Dave and Sid decided to make some beer that summer. They only drank beer when it was hot and they had been working hard, so they thought they could save some money by making their own. They would put it in the springhouse, which was a cellar-like place where the spring ran through it and kept the milk, butter, eggs and other perishables cool in the hot summer.

They went ahead and made the beer. I washed all the bottles and helped them cap them, and then we all lugged the beer to the springhouse and down the dirt steps into the cool darkness.

About a week later, I was hanging clothes on the line. By this time I had learned how to do the laundry the way a real farm wife should, so I was proud of my "white whites"; the dark jeans and denim work shirts all hung to dry in the South Dakota breeze. The dog and cat were helping me with this chore. All was quiet until there was suddenly what sounded like gunfire and a lot of it! It took me a minute to figure out that the beer must have exploded in the spring house, so I went there at top speed, and sure enough, each and every bottle had blown it's top. What a mess! The "free" supply of beer was all over everything. It took a long time to clean up because everything was ruined and we had no vacuum cleaner to help sweep up the shattered glass. That was a tedious job.

Dave's mother had a stroke, so we moved to her home so I could take care of her. They lived on a farm close to Sid's place, so Dave was able to keep working at Sid's. I would make Sid's lunch along with Dave's. Sid usually came home with Dave and ate dinner with us. He even trusted me to do his laundry!

It wasn't long before I got sick, and I do mean sick. If I moved from a laying down position, I threw up. Dave took good care of me and would feed me in bed. It didn't take long to figure out that I was pregnant with our first child. I was sick for a solid six months. Both our Moms were thrilled at the thought of a grandchild. When it was time to go to the hospital, I didn't waste any time, and I'm glad I didn't because Glenn was born just ten minutes after I got there!

Glenn was the light of our lives. I really enjoy kids and babies anyway, and to have my own to love and care for gave my life a whole new meaning. Glenn was walking at nine months and was potty trained not long after that.

Dave's mother improved so we were able to move to my uncle's dairy farm where we had a tiny, two-bedroom house of our own. In the summer, I would take Glenn, in his big-wheeled stroller to feed and milk the cows. Glenn loved just sitting and watching all the action. The old dog would always sit protectively by Glenn to guard him from danger.

We wanted our children to be about eighteen months apart, like my brother and me, so we decided to try for another baby. It wasn't long before I was pregnant again, but I kept right on riding my horse and milking the cows as long as I could. I had a hot, miserable summer, but in the fall I gave birth to a blond, blue eyed baby girl. Again, I barely made it to the hospital before Cindy was born. Dave was so proud of his little girl that he had wanted so badly.

Glenn liked to stay at my Mom and Dad's so he was there when his sister was born. He was his Grandma's pride and joy until the day she died. Glenn was born after my brother was in the Air Force, so my Mom had him in her life just as she really needed someone new to love and care for. Dave's mother had a fatal stroke and had passed away shortly after Glenn was born, so I think my Mom had decided she had to love and spoil him enough for both Grandmas. By this time, Grandpa Bryan was in poor health. He absolutely adored his great-grandson and enjoyed holding him in his lap as he sat in his easy chair.

When we took Cindy home from the hospital, and Glenn came home from his visit with my parents, we were a complete family. We were very happy; working hard and enjoying our life. We didn't have much money but we did a lot of fun things as a family that don't cost anything. We even had fun milking the cows!

Chapter 7

Dave got word that a rancher from Sundance, Wyoming was looking for a helper. The rancher raised registered horned Hereford cattle. Dave had always wanted to do that, so he applied for the job. When we learned that he got the job, we prepared to move to Sundance.

Of course, it was a new experience being away from my parents and from everything I grew up with, but we were excited about this new adventure, even if it was only thirty miles away from where I grew up.

When we got to Art and Olive Shelldorf's ranch, we learned that their son, Charles, had been killed when he was eleven by falling off the face of a mountain. We were told that Dave had a lot of the same characteristics as Charles, so it didn't take long for him, and us, to fit into their lives like a glove.

All these years later, I still visit Olive Shelldorf, whenever I get a chance. I call her often. Her health isn't very good at 96. She wanted me to move back to live with her but I couldn't leave my family and responsibilities here. But, she is welcome to move in with me any time.

We became like a big family, doing all the holidays together, working and playing together and depending on each other in good times and bad. It wasn't unusual for all of us to go dancing at an old, small schoolhouse near the ranch with the other people of the community.

Most of the ranchers held permits to take their cattle to the hills on National Forest land. I loved that time of year when the calves were all branded and the bull calves were castrated. The calves were all run through a chute and vaccinated, sprayed for insects and otherwise gotten ready for pasture.

About a week after we got done with those chores, the cattle were hauled to the hills. On the Shelldorf ranch we were only seven miles from the hills, so it was a short haul. I loved doing the work of herding cows and thought I could have done it my whole life.

The spring of 1959, Art's horse was lame so he had borrowed a horse from a neighbor. The one he borrowed was a big strawberry roan whose name was "Daisy" and she looked to be really slow.

Dave and Art had decided that I would be the one to ride Daisy and Dave would ride my horse, Smoky. Neither Smoky nor I were consulted on this decision!

Olive and I were drinking coffee while Art and Dave got everything ready. Olive had fixed lunches to put in the saddlebags. The sandwiches always ended up in pretty poor shape by mealtime, but it was something to eat.

Art came crashing into the kitchen with his spurs and chaps on. He told us that Dave was about to get killed trying to get his saddle onto Smoky. He raved on that I needed to get rid of that wild thing! I told him that it would be fine and I headed for the barn. Dave wasn't even a little pleased with my horse. He had been trying for 20 minutes to get the blankety blank blank saddle on that thrashing, flailing, squatting thing that I always rode.

Smoky calmed down as soon as he sensed that I was in the barn. I told Dave to just wait outside and that I would saddle Smoky. I went up to his head, which was tied by a halter to the post. I talked to him for a few minutes to calm him down, then kissed his velvety nose, and scratched between his ears a little.

It didn't take long for the fear to leave his eyes and the fear was replaced by the kind, soft brown that they usually were. I gently put the saddle blanket on him, then with the off stirrup hooked over the saddle horn, so it wouldn't hit him in the belly, I lifted Dave's heavy roping saddle onto his back as gently as I could. I reached under him to grab the cinches to tighten them up and after his bridle was on just right, I led him out to Dave who was waiting outside.

Art was shocked because there had been no commotion in the barn. Dave had to tighten the cinches a little more, then mounted up and we were ready to let the cattle out of their pens and get started on the long-awaited cattle drive.

Now, I wasn't a bit impressed with my mount. Old Daisy just plodded along behind the cows, half asleep.

It had rained the night before and there a few mud puddles along the way. The day was absolutely beautiful with all of nature in spring dress. No flowers were blooming yet, but they were budding, getting ready for one of the greatest show on earth, and another one of God's glorious works—wildflowers in the mountains.

After awhile, I crossed my feet on Daisy's hump and almost fell asleep myself. Suddenly, BANG! I found myself sitting I a mud puddle. Daisy had seen a calf head for the brush and she had come alive! She knew just what to do, with or without me. Dave and Art rode back to where I was and sat in their saddles having a good laugh at my predicament. Daisy came back to look at me, too, and it seemed like she enjoyed the joke, too! She was so big that Dave had to get off my horse to give me hand back up on Daisy.

I decided after that experience that she was a real cow horse after all and I had to change my attitude about her and her abilities. I didn't get blasé' anymore on that cattle drive!

Soon the cattle were in the hills. Lots of them had been there for many summers and knew exactly where they were. They were happy to be back in that good pasture. In the fall, some of the older cows would come back to the ranch before we went to bring them back.

Dave and Art worked hard with the cattle. When it was time to enter them into the stock show and go up for auction, they took all the prizes and brought top dollar at the stock sale. This was quite an accomplishment, and they were justifiably proud.

One day, Dave wanted me to help him rake the hay, which was drying so fast that he could just follow me with the baler. I was driving a little tractor with a side delivery rake. I could do a good job and go pretty fast. It wasn't long before I had to keep shifting down, and down, when I noticed that Dave had unhooked the tractor from the baler and was coming across the field really fast. I stopped to see what he wanted, and he asked me if I had bothered to look back--I did and one of the wheels had fallen off the rake. I had made a pretty mess of the rake and it looked like someone had plowed the field behind me for quite a ways. Now, to this day, when I mow my lawn or other work like that, I keep looking back!

By the time Dave got the mess straightened out, he had lost all the time he thought he would save by having me help him. It didn't stop the work though, and in the next few days, we put up a lot of hay bales.

Chapter 8

During the long, cold winters on the Shelldorf ranch there was a lot to do to taking care of the cattle and sheep. It seemed like when the baby calves and lambs were born, starting in February, it was always nasty weather.

Dave worked around the clock checking the livestock. Sometimes a cow or ewe needed help with birthing. He would often come home with little lambs that were orphans, or maybe the ewe had had triplets and could only care for two of them. Lots of times, my car was moved outside and our garage was turned into an orphanage for what we called "bum" lambs. Sometimes they would arrive almost frozen. Those little lambs were brought right into the house. It didn't matter how many came in, we put them on chairs and on the couch, or anywhere else we could find to get them warm.

I used heating pads, hot water bottles and lots of blankets to try to bring their body temperature up. I gave them milk with a little whiskey in it. They were fed this mixture in their bottles until they were able to stand up and show a little life. When they were able to walk and suck the bottle well, they were moved to the garage. We would make room in this "non-intensive care" area for the new arrivals.

Glenn, and even Cindy, who was only two at the time, was pressed into duty helping hold bottles, sometimes one in each hand, to feed the "bums". As the lambs grew stronger, they pulled harder on the bottle, and sometimes it was a struggle just to hold onto it sometimes.

The family dog even joined in the effort by licking and snuggling with the little lambs which was a great help in the healing and nurturing process.

I'm proud to say that not one of those lambs died, but all grew up to join the flock at the ranch. Art and Olive were so pleased with the great lamb crop. They had at least 30 more lambs than they had expected. I just couldn't have let them die, not if I could help it.

Chapter 9

We lived in a duplex on property that joined the ranch. Olive's Dad, Henry and his wife, Creta, lived in the other side of the duplex. We became great friends and spent a lot of evenings together playing cards or sharing stories.

Henry was pretty hard of hearing and when he was going to town, or anywhere else, I always knew it. His car sounded like every rod in the engine would come flying out at any second when Henry raced his engine.

One day he was going to town and wondered why everyone was flailing their arms and blinking their lights at him. I'm sure they were honking their horns, but Henry wouldn't have heard them. He got to the store and opened his door. Then, he saw a cat running full bore down the street. That poor cat had had her tail caught in the door and had no claws or pads left on her front feet. I'm sure that the cat was screaming all the way. The cat made it back home before Henry did. Creta and I took her to the vet and she did recover, even though she was permanently declawed.

Our family and the Shelldorfs took trips together for hunting and fishing. We liked to go to Meadow Lakes Resort, in the Big Horn Mountains of Wyoming, to hunt and fish. One particular time, we were getting ready to go on an elk hunt and Art and Dave had set up a hay bale with a target for practice. I couldn't even hit the target which was standing still, so Dave told me that when we got to our hunting stations, that he didn't want me to shoot at anything, until he got his elk, as I would just scare them all off.

We got to our hunting ground and Dave got me settled in my station on a hill, again warning me not to shoot until he got his. He went on to his hunting station, on a nearby hill.

It wasn't long before it sounded like a bulldozer was coming through the woods. It was elk! I could hear Dave empty his gun, but the elk kept coming. So, in spite of what he had told me, I just took a shot, and the big bull fell in a heap of rubble! I threw my gun down and immediately ran down to where the elk lay. Needless to say, I didn't even have a knife. Dave was screaming and yelling at me to stop, but I kept ongoing. The big bull was dead. DEAD! I had shot him right under the ear! We didn't waste any of that meat!

When we got back to the camp and had the elk cooling, we went to the lodge to have dinner and celebrate. Art, Olive, Dave and I had each gotten an elk, but mine was the biggest! Dave never took me hunting again.

Chapter 10

When we recovered from the excitement of the elk hunt and the success of the cattle drive, I discovered that I was pregnant again. We had only planned on one boy and one girl, and thought that was a big enough family. But, here I was pregnant again. It took us awhile to be happy about this unexpected pregnancy, but we settled into the idea that our family would be bigger than we had planned.

This time, I wasn't sick, so the time flew by and before I knew it, I went into labor. Unlike the previous quick deliveries, this time the labor went on and on. I couldn't help but wonder if I was being punished for not wanting this baby at first. I remember overhearing the doctor say that they would "never get this baby out of her". Then, I went through a tunnel of lights. When I woke up, I thought I was in an insane asylum. The wallpaper looked to me like padding on the walls. It took me awhile to recover. To this day, Rick has a spot of fuzzy gray hair on his head from the effects of the forceps they used to help in his birth. The poor little guy was really beat up! We named him "Rick" and he had brown eyes and almost black hair

When we got Rick home, we learned that he got asthma from milk, so we had to feed him soybean formula. Rick was then, and still is a real blessing and was welcomed with open arms into our family. We didn't fully realize then what a true blessing all three of our children would prove to be as time went on.

All my three of my babies were just over six pounds, but Rick had been caught in my torn uterus. After his birth, I had to get a D&C and blood transfusions every month. This went on until Rick was a year old, and I finally went to another doctor, who insisted that I have a hysterectomy. The new doctor was absolutely shocked that I had been in this condition since giving birth a year before.

Mom and Dad had made a down payment on a house for us. Because of both Rick's and my health difficulties, a house was chosen close to the hospital. We really missed our ranch life and we saw the Shelldorfs often. Dave became a truck driver for awhile, then took a job at the Belle Fouche livestock exchange. It wasn't long before I started running the restaurant at the stock exchange.

We thoroughly enjoyed the sale barns. I had the cafe at the one in St. Onge and the one in Belle Fouche. Mom, Dad, Dave and I also ran the truck stop at the South end of Belle Fouche, too. We had a drive-in restaurant and a banquet room that my Dad had built on to the building. We catered a lot of big events, too. So, we managed to stay very busy!

Dave and I, Rick, Cindy and Glenn after a family outing

Glenn, Cindy and Rick were used to helping themselves to candy and other goodies at our places. Once, though, we were out of town and had to stop for gas. Of course, the kids had to go to the bathroom, and then they just slid open the door of the showcase for candy like they did at home.

Dave and the station attendant went in just as this was happening. They got a lecture that they still remember about the rules being different when it's not your family's place, or if you don't have permission to just help yourself.

Chapter 11

Dave and I were very happy in our marriage. We respected, as well as loved, each other, and we had fun together. Until the day he died, Dave always called me "Bubbles". We had three wonderful children who were as near perfect as any three children can be. Glenn and Cindy never fought much, but the two of them picked on Rick a lot.
One evening I came home from work to find Rick crying under the kitchen table. Glenn and Cindy had told him that he was adopted. They got into big trouble for that!

Since Rick was so much younger than the other two, he went to the sale barn with me when Glenn and Cindy were in school. He liked to wear his silver spurs, cowboy hat, jeans and fringed leather jacket. . Of course, all the farmers and ranchers got to know him and liked to call him "Little Festus" in his fancy outfit.

"Little Festus"

Dave worked in the stockyard where the livestock was penned until they were sold, or loaded onto the train, or trucks, to be delivered to the buyer.

Like all working mothers, I had to tend to the chores at home the best I could. One of the chores I hated above all others was ironing, and I didn't care who knew how much I hated it.

One afternoon, Dave came home while I was ironing. He came over to me and told me to give him the basket of clothes I was working on. He told me that he had found a lady to do the ironing for me, and that he'd rather pay her, and does the delivery and pick up than to have to live with me while I ironed. Needless to say, I didn't question his judgment on that decision! She did a beautiful job

Chapter 12

In the late spring of 1965, there was a demolition derby at the local fairgrounds. We had just moved to a new house a few blocks away and decided to go to the race. Rick was sick so he had to stay home with the baby-sitter.

We had a pet skunk named "Inky". He was used to all the dogs in our old neighborhood, but he hadn't gotten used to the dogs where we had moved. Our old boxer dog "Old Duke" had adopted Inky. Inky slept between Old Duke's legs. Rick and the baby-sitter had both been warned to not take Inky outside.

Despite the warning, Rick took Inky out and a dog killed Inky! All the kids cried all night.

Dave had to go out on a trip driving truck the next day, so I took the kids to a pet shop in Deadwood to look for a new skunk. They didn't have any skunks, but they had the cutest chimpanzee I had ever seen. So, we bought the chimp and named her "Patty". Patty liked to play with the kids all the time. She would jump up and grab the boys' short butch haircuts and that would start a wrestling match. Our kids charged the neighbor kids a nickel to play with their chimp!

Patty was scared of Old Duke. When the dog came to the screen door, she was instantly climbed the drapes. This activity went on for a couple of weeks while Dave was on his road trip. One night he got home about 2:00 a.m. and went straight to bed. When he got up, he told us that he had had the strangest dream; he had dreamed that there was a monkey sitting on the dresser! Of course, it wasn't a dream, and it didn't take me long to figure out that Dave wouldn't accept a monkey of any kind in our house. So, when the kids got home from school, we took Patty to the Hill City Zoo.

Word got around to Dave's trucking buddies and they all gave him a really bad time over the monkey. Eventually all they had to do was mention the word "monkey" and Dave would come unglued. His buddies must have liked to upset him, because they kept it up for a long time.

Russell Backhaus and Dave Dilley

Chapter 13

After that experience, I decided to invest in horses instead of monkeys. We made extra money training the young, unbroken horses. Dave could break them very well. But, the ones I broke turned out to be strictly for women, and the men couldn't ride them at all. Once, I bought a little black half Welsh and half quarter-horse pony. He turned out to be the fastest pony in the county.

All the time, I was still working at the sale barn and I liked to work the horses there where the pen fences were high. I had good help who would give me a couple of hour's break from cooking so that I could pen cattle with the horse I was working with at the time.

A rancher from Camp Crook, South Dakota, tried to buy "Coalie", the little Welsh pony, from me for a long time. I finally had to give up and sell him when he offered me so much that I couldn't refuse. That rancher's grandson won every race in the country on Coalie. The boy was a good little rider and he had the best pony by far.

Chapter 14

Dave had dreamed about moving to Alaska for a long time. His sister, Betty, and her family, had been in Alaska for over a year, and loved it. Dave and I had talked about joining them, and finally, an opportunity came to do just, that, and we jumped at the chance.

In preparation for the move, we had a big auction sale to get rid of almost all we owned. The rule was that if it wouldn't fit in the travel trailer we were taking on the move, it went into the sale. As I sorted through what to keep and what to sell, I really had mixed emotions about the move. I loved the life I had, but shared Dave's excitement about a new adventure. The kids were all torn also, looking forward to the new, but having a really hard time telling their friends good-bye. Glenn was twelve, Cindy ten and Rick seven and they had formed some solid friendships. But, they were also at the perfect age to look forward to and enjoy the new, big adventure, of moving so far away from all that they had ever known. My Mom stayed behind in South Dakota to take care of our restaurants until we could get settled and Dad had work.

We had a station wagon to pull the travel trailer, and all the space we had was crammed full of people, Dave and me, our three children, Donnie Barnes, and my Dad. Not to mention our big, old, boxer dog, Duke! The cat had to ride in the travel trailer. Dave's Dad was following behind us in his car. All of us would take turns riding with him, getting a break from the crowded station wagon. He only had room for one passenger because his car was loaded, too.

The roads were in good shape, so we made time at an acceptable rate. But it was the first part of April and there was still deep snow in the Canadian wilderness. We had noticed a sign warning all travelers to put on chains, but the road was good and we ignored the warning. We didn't get much farther before we jackknifed the travel trailer on an icy, steep curve in the middle of nowhere, going over a pass. We weren't too worried about anyone coming along and hitting us, but on the other hand, we couldn't be sure!

Suddenly, Glenn said he thought he heard a sound like a Jake brake on a truck! Then, we were certain we could hear him coming, but couldn't tell for sure from which direction! That meant we weren't as safe as we thought we might be. Talk about a mad scramble! Dave's Dad took his car back down the road to try to warn the truck driver, in case it was coming that way. The rest of us made our way up the hill to try to warn the truck driver about our plight if he were coming in that direction..

We soon knew for sure that he was coming down the steep and winding road. We got his attention and he was able to get stopped in time, or he would have smashed us good! The truck driver was prepared for emergencies and had a winch on his truck, which he used to pull us out of our predicament. You'd better believe that Dave took the time right then and there and put the chains on the rig while we all kept our lookout posts for more traffic. Thank God for that truck driver!

After that experience, we traveled all day with white knuckles over that mountain pass.

At the end of the day, we found a motel, and it's a good thing we weren't too choosy! The beds sagged and there was no hot water. When we found the eating place, the kitchen was closed, so we had to settle for a cold cheese sandwich and potato chips. We were so exhausted, we didn't care, so after we finished our "meal" we made plans for sleeping arrangements.

Donnie always slept in the travel trailer. Fortunately it was a good thing that he was good-natured. Remember that we had a cat traveling in the travel trailer, so, of course, it had to have kitty litter. The problem was that the cat would dig in the kitty litter all night long--probably for something to do--and keep Donnie awake all night. You would think that Donnie would have taken the chance to have a turn at a bed instead of listening to the cat, but took one look at the sagging bed and decided the cat was better. The cat certainly didn't snore anyway!

As we went on our way, we stopped one morning at a lodge for breakfast and decided to order pancakes for breakfast because they were cheap. Well, when we got them, they were about as round as a silver dollar and paper thin. By the time we filled up the whole crew, they were not cheap! (As a reminder to someone reading this who is thinking about traveling that road, be assured that in the thirty one years since we made the trip, the road has improved tremendously and the motels and restaurants are first class now)

When we finally crossed the line into Alaska, we thought we should be close to the end of our trip, but it seemed like it took forever to get the rest of the way to Anchorage. Of course, we had had visions of pristine snow and beauty everywhere. Although we were horrified at the dirty snow along the road, when we looked at the mountains, they were absolutely majestic and so awesome. I felt so close to God because it was obvious that He had made the mountains.

At long last, we arrived in Anchorage and found Dave's sister and her family. They lived on the southwest side of Anchorage at the corner of Dimond Blvd. and Kincaid. What a relief! Betty fixed a real feast for us and we all took hot showers for the first time in days. We unloaded the travel trailer enough to live in but it only took one night for me to decide that I'm not cut out to be a camper!

In the morning, no one could move until everyone stood up and made their beds and pushed them back. I had to turn our bed into the dining room table. Then, we could get to the bathroom. If everyone else sat down, I could make breakfast. My disposition was not the best in those cramped quarters and it didn't take long for the whole crew to learn to go through the routine without protest.

The second day, Dave and I went looking for a lot to put a mobile home on. While we were looking around, we went up the mountainside to what we call 'Upper Hillside" in Anchorage. The view of Cook Inlet, the mountains, and Anchorage was absolutely breathtaking. But, the snow was still deep in that area and the roads were very scary.

We finally found lots for sale near Betty and Loren. We picked out two that were on a hill with a view of the mountains. In two weeks, we were perched on top with the ugliest mobile home you ever saw. We had traded our new, beautiful travel trailer for that monster, but at least we could move around in it.

We all got busy and worked on clearing the brush on the lot, working on fixing the mobile home, getting the yard planted and making arrangements for all the utilities to be brought in. We were exhausted but in heaven.

The guys were all looking for work, but couldn't find a job, so I went to work baking at Elmendorf Air Force Base, and also found a part time job at a Mexican restaurant and also a few hours a week at the grocery store. Dave, our Dads and Donnie were all used to working hard, and it didn't set well with them that at first I was the only one who could get work, but it didn't take long before they were all working, too.

When school started, I got a job as a cook for the hot lunch program at Dimond High School. The hours were perfect since I was at home at the same times the kids were, and had summers and holidays off with them. Dave and Donnie were driving trucks, so they weren't home much. My Dad was working in Soldotna. Dave's Dad, Jake, had gone back to South Dakota once he helped get us all settled. The kids had all made friends and were busy in their lives. Everyone was happy.

It wasn't long before my best friend, Darlene Barnes, joined her husband, Donnie, in Alaska. She remembered how much I hated to iron, so she did it for me! In return, I cleaned her house--anything but ironing! Of course, I did it when I had to.

Chapter 15

One beautiful summer day in 1970 we went for a drive to Palmer and up the road to Fairbanks for a ways. On the drive, we could see Mount McKinley, a masterpiece of God, really well. The mountain was so big and majestic the way the sun reflected on the snow, making it a pale pink (which we call "alpenglow"). I truly believe that God has a perfect color scheme in His creation that we enjoy.

We turned onto the Hatcher Pass Road, which goes up into the Talkeetna Mountains into the area where gold was discovered in the late 1800's. The road was just a trail as we neared the top. But, with the roaring creek and the view, it was gorgeous. We parked the car and hiked and played around in the creek. On our way home, we noticed a "land for sale" sign at milepost 56 of the Anchorage to Fairbanks Highway (the George Parks Highway). Glenn commented that we should look into buying land in that area. There was a beautiful view of Mount McKinley there, too.

We decided to look into it and ended up buying 70 acres, just off the highway, from Rose Palmquist. Rose had homesteaded that property in the late 1950's and had just sold the front 40 acres with the house and barn to someone else the day before. We were happy with the 70 acres, which was like a park with huge spruce and birch trees.

When the Alaska Railroad was built, about 1915, the trees in the area had been burned, but the trees on the 70 acres we had just purchased, had been spared. They were absolutely beautiful. There was deep moss underfoot and not a lot of underbrush, so it was like walking through a park when we wandered in the woods.

As often as we could on weekends, we would load our two horses, a little motorcycle and the kids and go to the property. It was only 56 miles from downtown Anchorage, but the difference was like we were a million miles away. In the summer, we liked to ride our horses, play on the motorcycle and just explore.

A gravel pit had been dug out, about a half mile from our property, when they had built the highway. It was also close to the Little Susitna River, and water had accumulated in the gravel pit. It made a perfect "bath tub" for us. After we got done playing, we would take our bar of soap and have a bath--clothes and all! We felt cleaner, but whether we looked or smelled better, may be a question!

In the winter, we took snowmachines and rode through the property and along the many trails that run through the region. Once, we had too many kids with us for everyone to have a spot on the snowmachines, so I volunteered to ride in the sled. My seat was an old, rusty bucket.

We were riding (actually bouncing) along the power line, with all the humps and ridges which were left there either by an earthquake or by glaciers. The snowmachines were all being ridden very fast so that they sailed through the air when they hit these bumps. Believe me, my "bucket seat" had no cushion, and by the time we got back home, I had a bruised seat!

One time I was riding behind Dave, and while he was enjoying "catching air" on his jump, the tongue on the sled twisted and the sled toppled onto it's side. My bucket seat also toppled over, and I just hung on for dear life, even though I was being dragged along. I didn't see the humor in it that everyone else seemed to be enjoying.

Over the years, we spent many happy weekends there, always with a dream of eventually moving to the property. We visualized our horses grazing in the pasture, putting up hay from the fields and just enjoying the country life full time.

Chapter 16

Later that same year, a horse sale was advertised at Elmendorf Air Force Base, where they were selling some of the "dude" horses. There was nothing in the notice that indicated that these horses might be only for very experienced riders.

So, I took my two nieces, Rhoda and Carla Dodds, my nephew, Kent Dodds, three neighbor kids, and my three kids to inspect the horses.

When we got to the gate at the military base, we had to stop to get a permit to enter. The guard asked me how many people were in the car and I told him I had nine kids plus myself. He said that that was two people too many. So, I told him that we were going to the horse sale and asked him which two kids he wanted to watch while we were there! He gave me a permit and told me that I'd better not do anything to get stopped by the M.P.s. So, I proceeded very, very carefully to the stables.

About the third horse we looked at was a dappled, dark colored palomino that Cindy wanted. He was a beautiful quarter horse. So, I got him for her and she named him "Ringo". After we looked at about ten more horses, they brought out a chestnut thoroughbred. He was a fine looking animal. I bought him and called him "Jiggs".

Now, I had no clue about how I would get the horses home. I called a doctor friend who had a stable on O'Malley Road in Anchorage. He assured me that it would be no problem for him to pick them up for me.

So, about 6:00 p.m. that same evening, the horses arrived. It didn't take us long to figure out that they weren't safe to ride. They were so spoiled by the "dudes" that we had to rebreak them to be ridden properly.

If Ringo was tied, he tried his best to break whatever was confining him. One day, I took Dave's lariat and placed it around Ringo's flanks, through his halter, and between his front legs, then tied him with the rope to a big birch tree.

I went to the house and soon heard a big commotion outside. Ringo tried, as usual, to break loose, but that time, he was fooled. The rope around his flanks got tighter when he fought it, and I do mean tight!

Cindy was crying because I was hurting her horse. I told her that he was doing it to himself and he would stop when he figured that out. Then, he wouldn't be breaking halters and bridles anymore.

Jiggs would run backward when you tried to get on him, so it was impossible for me to get on him bareback. When Dave came home, he put a saddle on Jiggs, and took him to a burned out cabin nearby. The foundation hole was still there. Dave placed Jiggs so that when he ran backward, he would end up in the hole. So, as soon as Dave got his foot in the stirrup, Jiggs started his high-gear reverse maneuver.

Dave stepped out of the stirrup, and Jiggs tumbled backward into the foundation hole. That was all that it took.

After those incidents, both Ringo and Jiggs gave our family lots of riding fun. We took them with us when we went to our seventy acres in the summer. Glenn always took his motorcycle. He and Rick weren't much into horses but Rick always rode with me on Jiggs. Our family enjoyed exploring the back trails all over God's beautiful country. Even as we ducked and dodged trees and other obstacles along the way, we thoroughly enjoyed those outings.

We plowed some of the cleared land to plant oats for our horses. Of course, Dave was doing the plowing and the kids and I were hauling rocks. We would just get an armful of rocks picked up and had started across the rough plowed ground when the mosquitoes attacked us.

It was worth it, because the oat crop turned out good. But, Dave decided to get some more hay while the oats finished developing. So, we bought some hay from John C., Dave's old boss at Soldotna.

Dave had a half-ton pickup and had built a big trailer to haul hay and other stuff. Coming back from Soldotna, our six-cylinder pickup would barely make some of the big hills. The trailer was so loaded with hay that the front wheels of the truck were barely touching the ground. After that trip, we decided we needed a one ton truck. Dave came home one day with a Chevy flatbed that he could build a stock rack on, and we used that truck to go to rodeos.

Chapter 17

My parents were living in Soldotna, on the Kenai Peninsula, about a three-hour trip the opposite direction from Anchorage than our property. The Kenai Peninsula is world-famous for salmon fishing and for the glorious scenery. Their home was built really close to the Kenai River, which is a magnet for salmon fishermen.

When we didn't go north to our property, the kids and I often left on Friday afternoons as soon as we got off work and school to spend the weekend with my parents on the Kenai Peninsula. One weekend, the kids wanted to spend the night in a sheep wagon on "John C's" sheep ranch. Rick liked to go fishing, so he left to go fishing and came back with three very small fish that he was very proud of and insisted that I cook for his dinner.

The sheep wagon only had a little wood stove, but between us, we got it fired up and ready to fix our meal. It was summer and the sheep wagon was very small, so it didn't take long for it to get awfully hot inside the wagon. Even leaving the window open didn't help much, but we decided it was worth the discomfort for Rick to have his delicacies. He did enjoy what little bit he could pick off the bones.

Dave came down later and we all went out to dinner in town. Rick always had to have steamed clams, even though I could hardly stand the look or smell of the things. It was obvious that his big feast of fish hadn't put much of damper on his appetite!

We enjoyed our evening as a family and eventually went back to the ranch to spend the night in the sheep wagon. Because the cooking fire had made it so hot, we had left the window open to air it out while we were gone. But, we had failed to notice that the window had no screen, so the infamous Alaskan mosquitoes had made themselves at home, and the place was absolutely full of the pests!

Needless to say, we spent that night listening to buzzing and trying to keep them away from our ears. The bed wasn't the most comfortable either, but the kids enjoyed themselves anyway and talked for a long time about their night in a sheep wagon.

We spent the next night at Mom and Dad's! We made it a practice to go there as many weekends as we could, and the boys caught some beautiful fish in the Kenai River.

I never could catch a salmon there. It seemed like people all around me were pulling in fish. I would trade spots and still no bites. It really didn't matter though, because I enjoyed just being outside with my family and enjoying the fantastic scenery.

On Sunday afternoons, we headed home to Anchorage. Mountains were on both sides of the road and the road went for miles along Cook Inlet. Portage Glacier was visible from the highway in those days. Occasionally we saw whales in the inlet and we often saw many wild ducks and geese in the marshy areas. It was always a tiring ride back to Anchorage after our busy weekend of fun.

We lived in the mobile home for three years while we built our new house on an adjoining lot. We finally finished and got moved in for Christmas 1972. To this day, I can't stand tomato soup and grilled cheese sandwiches--I had them too many times while we were building our house!

We really enjoyed the view of the mountains. It was a nice big house and each of the kids each had a big bedroom and we had a big rec.room that was always busy with our kids and their many friends.

We always told the kids what our money situation was. Sometimes movies and other treats were out of the question, but they could always have their friends at our house. It wasn't unusual to have sixteen kids at our house at once. At least I always knew where my kids were, whom they were with and what they were doing.

There was never a shortage of food to feed my family and their friends. My Mom was amazed at how I did it, until I reminded her that she had done the same thing when Chuck and I were growing up.

Chapter 18

But, by 1971, my Dad had developed some health problems and was in a lot of pain. Both his hands and arms were numb. After months and months of going from doctor to doctor, he ended up having a test where they shoot dye into the body then trace it's path by turning the patient upside down. Through this process they found a liquid cyst inside his spinal cord, which stretched from the base of his brain to where his neck connected to his shoulders.

They had to do a dangerous operation to drain the fluid out. The doctor told us that it was entirely possible that Dad would never draw another breath.

The night of this serious surgery I had another vision, or nightmare. About 4:00 a.m. I sat up in bed. My heart was pounding. The headless man was standing by my bed again.

Dave woke up, too, and wanted to know what was wrong. For a while, I couldn't answer him. I was seeing the beautiful golden, spiral, staircase again.

I was finally able to tell Dave, in a shaky voice, that I thought Dad had just died. We called the hospital and talked to the nurse and were assured that Dad was still alive and in critical, but stable, condition.

I got up and Dave made some good, strong, coffee for us. Then, about an hour later the phone rang. It was Dad's sister on the phone. Her husband, Uncle Leonard, had been killed when his mechanical "farmhand", loaded with hay, had tipped over, and Uncle Leonard's head was under it.

Dad was so bad that Mom couldn't go to be with Aunt Marie, so Dave and I went to be with her. We were her only family. We stayed a week after the funeral to help her take care of things and get reorganized.

Our friend, Russell Backhaus went to stay with Mom and take her back and forth to the hospital to be with Dad. Dad lived another five years after that. (Thank goodness that Russell was home from the North Slope and could step in for us at this time that we needed him so much.)

Dave arranged to sell Uncle Leonard's cows. Aunt Marie was a schoolteacher and couldn't handle all the heavy work taking care of the cattle. Thank goodness that my beloved aunt had wonderful neighbors who stepped in to care for her.

Chapter 19

One day in July 1972, the Matanuska-Susitna Borough, which is similar to a county, was having a land sale and property close to ours in Houston was listed in the auction. Dave Coker (we called him "Coker" to avoid confusion with Dave), and Donnie and Darlene Barnes were interested in buying a parcel. So, the weekend before the sale was scheduled, Darlene, her mother, all six of Darlene's kids, Glenn, Cindy and Rick, Coker and I went to our place to camp and to look over the property which was listed for sale.

There were a few swamps in between the properties, so we took the hunting rig, which could usually navigate through swamps without trouble. After we pitched a big tent, we set out on the hunting rig to explore the area.

Coker had to drive, and at one point he got stuck. We all hopped off the rig, into the deep muck, to push. We were finally successful and went on our way. The countryside was absolutely beautiful (except for the mosquitoes, which had sent out an abundant welcoming committee). We saw moose, squirrels, spruce hens, rabbits, and all sorts of birds.

We finally went back to our place to finish setting up camp. It wasn't long before we had the camp stove going and heated up the stew and rolls I had brought with us. We finished off with chocolate cake.

Darlene's station wagon made a good bedroom for her mother and the little boys
The rest of us took our sleeping bags into the big tent and chose our spot for the night. With the crew we had, there wasn't an extra spot on the floor by the time we all got our bedrolls laid out. We peeked outside the tent and noticed that after the beautiful day, it was starting to cloud up.

Soon after climbing into the sleeping bags, Coker started snoring. Then, we thought we heard a bear scratching and clawing at the tent. By that time, it had started raining. About 1:00 a.m., Darlene decided she had to ventured outside to the "bathroom". She wanted me to go with her, so I took my flashlight and machete, to protect us from all that might want to harm us.

We were wet by that time, and the wind had come up pretty strongly. While Darlene was tending to her business, I checked the tent and discovered that the "bear" was really a branch blowing in the wind and rubbing against the tent.

Coker's snoring hadn't slowed down any. Darlene had yet to close one eye when the boys from the station wagon came running, hollering all the way that there were two abominable snowmen out by the station wagon. We guessed that they hadn't gotten very much sleep either! After careful investigation, we determined that the abominable snowmen turned out to be the neighbor's Holstein cows! The boys went back to the station wagon and Darlene and I stuffed our now-wet bodies back into the sleeping bags. I think that we may have gotten a couple of hours sleep the whole night.

Then, we got up early to start cooking lots of bacon for the crew. Pretty soon, Coker stumbled out of the tent, grumbling that he hadn't gotten any sleep! We told him the events of the night and how his snoring had contributed to the uproar. He had been totally unaware that anything exciting had happened!

After we filled our bellies with bacon, eggs and pancakes, we quickly took the tent down and headed back to Anchorage and real beds. We still remember those abominable snowmen!

In spite of all that effort, neither Coker nor the Barnes bought any property at the auction. They thought the price was too high. But, ever since, they've been sorry they passed up that opportunity.

Chapter 20

In the spring of 1973, we went to Seattle and bought Dave a new pickup truck, then went on to South Dakota. While we were on that trip, Dave bought a beautiful Appaloosa horse. Of course, we had to buy a horse trailer, too. We also got a Chinese pug puppy, which we named "McDonald". We had a great time on what turned out to be our last vacation together.

That same spring, Olive Shelldorf came to Alaska to see us and we decide to take Olive to Dawson City in Canada. We put the camper on Dave's new pick up, loaded the kids and McDonald and took off. When we got to the Canadian border, the border guard asked us if we had brought the proper papers to allow the dog to enter Canada. Of course we didn't! So, the man had to look at McDonald, and when he saw him, he told us that our dog was "just like the Queen's dog" and that of course it was O.K. to enter Canada.

The view from the Top of the World Highway was spectacular. We could see for miles and miles--the far away rivers and mountains were glorious and breathtaking. Also breathtaking were the old wrecked cars, pickup toppers and camper trailers that had rolled off the road, through carelessness or accidents.

When we got to the Yukon River, we took a ferry across. We drove right onto the ferry. The river was big and wide and the ride was smooth. When we got to the other side, we drove off the ferry and into Dawson City.

While we were there, we panned for gold and went to Diamond Lil's. Rick almost lost his eyeballs when he saw the girls as they danced and high-kicked their way through the evening. It was a great show.

By the time the show was over, it was late, so we went to the campground and to bed. We had just gotten to sleep when someone banged on the door and tried to open it. Thank heaven, we had a secure lock, because the person kept banging and banging, insisting that someone named "Bob" was inside. Dave tried to explain that we had no one named "Bob" in our camper and that he had the wrong camper. (I think he'd tipped one too many at Diamond Lil's). Needless to say, we didn't get much sleep that night. In spite of that, the trip to Dawson City was great and I'd recommend it to anyone.

On the way home, Olive and Rick wanted to pan for gold. They had spotted a likely looking creek, so we stopped. While I fixed lunch, Dave, Olive, Rick and, of course, McDonald, were busy with their gold pans. They came back all excited with their success at gold panning. We soon found out that it was fool's gold. It shines so bright in the clear streams along the road. They still had a great time and were excited for awhile.

Chapter 21

Too soon, we were home in Anchorage and Dave had to go back to work. Olive stayed for quite a bit longer, and we had a lot of good times together. One day, we decided to get dressed up for a fancy lunch at a downtown fancy restaurant. So, we got ready and decided to drive around and look at the sights before going to lunch. We ended up at Ship Creek. The tides come in that beautiful little creek and make it much larger than when the tide is out. The salmon come in from the ocean and up the creek. In June the big king salmon return to their spawning grounds.

Olive and I decided to watch the big ones jump as they swam up the face of the little dam on the creek. What a sight those huge, glistening fish make when they make their big struggle to get over the dam. They would keep trying, tails working to propel them but some couldn't do it. It wasn't long before three fellows from the Department of Fish and Game came and pulled his water tank truck onto the grid, which was part way onto the dam.

We watched as the king salmon went into the fish trap, which was right under the grid. The fish that went that way were trapped. While we watched, we saw some men put a liquid into the water to tranquilize the fish. It wasn't long before the men reached into the water and started pulling the huge fish out of the trap and putting them into a water tank on the back of the truck.

Now, remember that we were dressed up for our lunch, with our fancy dresses and high heeled shoes. When they were in the process of pulling a fish out of the water, there was a lot of thrashing and splashing. Soon, we were more than a little wet! The makeup we had so carefully put on for our fancy lunch was washing away. But we could have cared less. Not very many people get to observe the operation we were seeing.

We found out that they were capturing the king salmon to take to the hatchery, where they milked them, by squeezing the eggs from the females and the semen from the males. They would then raise the fertilized eggs to the point that they could be released back to the ocean to start the cycle all over again. We watched the men the whole time they were there, then walked up and down the creek to dry off a bit. Then, we took our fishy, messed up, selves to a wonderful lunch. The waiters didn't seem to notice, or if they did, they were too polite to let us know!

Chapter 22

My husband made it back home in a few days and we went halibut fishing in Homer. The drive to Homer was just perfect. The Dall sheep were on the mountains by Kenai Lake. We saw mama moose with their young babies. Volcanoes were shining red and gold across Cook Inlet. We stopped at Clam Gulch and dug a few clams. Olive had never done that before.

We showed her how to get on the ocean side with your little shovel and watch for what looks like someone stuck a pencil in the ground. Not wasting a second, you dig like fury with your clam shovel, then throw your shovel down and use your hands to dig in the sand. Using this method, we usually ended up with a clam. Since we only wanted a few clams, we didn't stay there long.

We could feel God's presence in this spectacular spot that He had made. The volcanoes stood proud across the glistening water. The bluff we had climbed down was aglow with the evening sun.

We got to Homer late, and didn't get much sleep as our halibut charter left at six o'clock the next morning. After a big breakfast, we met our skipper at the dock, then lugged our equipment aboard his nifty boat, and were off. We went a long ways out in the water before the skipper stopped the boat and told us to fish. The ocean was like glass and the sun was shining, putting out warmth and light. Soon we were catching big halibut. Rick caught the first one, but Olive caught the biggest one. She was so tickled! Her fish weighed 89 pounds. Now, that's a lot of fish!

We cruised back to the dock, where we still had to filet and get the fish on ice and ready to take home. After the long drive back, we had to freeze the bounty. It was another short night! But, in June in Alaska, it's light most of the time, and it seems like it's never time to go to bed anyway.

Dave had to leave on another long haul the next day and Olive would be leaving at 12:30 the next morning. We had had a wonderful time. I'm so glad, because the good times were almost over. God had another plan coming up.

Cindy was the only one of the kids who got to go with us to pick up Dave's new truck in Seattle and a vacation in South Dakota, since Glenn had to work and Rick stayed with Mom and Dad in Soldotna, so that he could fish. Mom was the main cook at the hospital in Soldotna, so Rick went to work with Dad. There was a little creek close by Dad's work place, so Rick spent every day fishing while Dad worked. Then, in the evenings, the two of them went fishing in the Kenai River, which is big and swift.

We always had lots of fun as a family, even if we didn't have much money. We went snowmachining, skiing, and fishing, horseback riding, or just went to the lake for a picnic.

Dave did have a temper, and once in a while it would flare up. It would show itself when I was driving, and managed to get stuck. He got upset because he didn't think I could drive right. One particular night it snowed and he couldn't get his pickup out. It was a Saturday and I didn't have to go to work. So, when he couldn't get his pickup out, he came in the house and accused me of parking my car in the wrong place. He informed me that he was going to take my car and that I would be on foot all day.

Well, I have a temper that explodes once in awhile, too! So, I told him to go ahead and take my car, but not to bother to come home. About 6:00 p.m., I was in the kitchen, and I noticed Dave's old, red cap come sailing into the kitchen while he crawled in on his hands and knees. We both started laughing. We never stayed mad at each other.

We made it a point to never go to bed angry with each other. Our life together was just perfect most of the time.

Dave worked hard as a truck driver. He took the first truck load of equipment to the North Slope to use in developing the Prudhoe Bay oil field. He was part of a "Cat train". They even drove over glaciers. It was very dangerous. At that time, he was working for John C. Miller (Frontier Rock and Sand) and hauled loads from the Lower 48, also. He hauled longhorn cattle from Texas; sheep from Montana, Tennessee walking horses from John C's horse farm in Tennessee to his ranch in Soldotna.

My Dad worked on John C.'s ranch, mostly rebuilding the antique wagons and farm equipment that Dave had hauled up from the lower 48. Dave even hauled a crane from Pennsylvania!

On one trip, he was hauling Tennessee walking horses and decided to let them rest, feed and water, in Belle Fouche. The kids and I flew down and met them there. We were there over the 4th of July, so decided to ride those horses in the Belle Fouche 4th of July parade. Those farmers and ranchers had never seen anything like those horses. They were absolutely beautiful to look at, but worthless as working cow horses.

While we were there, we enjoyed the rodeo very much. Rodeos in Alaska were just starting and weren't nearly as exciting as what we'd been used to in South Dakota.

Art and Olive Shelldorf came over from Sundance, Wyoming to join us and to see Cindy. They were like another Grandpa and Grandma to our kids. Glenn had had to stay in Alaska to work. Coker and his wife had stayed at our house to take Rick fishing while we were gone.

Rick was really happy about that arrangement, and I thought I was, too. But that was before we got home and found that the basement was so stinky we couldn't stand it. We set about searching for the problem and found it--under Rick's bed. He had stored a bucket full of salmon eggs under there to save for bait. He had forgotten to salt them, and they had been there way too long! It took a long time to get the stink out the house. I haven't still haven't figured out how Rick could stand to sleep in that bed with that smell under it!

We made it a point to go to South Dakota at least once a year to see our relatives, but couldn't wait to get back to beautiful Alaska. There is something special about this state that makes a person feel much closer to God.

Chapter 23

In 1973, Dave had made arrangements to cut hay on the bluff near the intersection of the Glenn and Parks Highways (about 35 miles north of Anchorage). So, when he came home from a trucking run, we went to put up hay. Dave mowed the hay and while it was drying a little, Cindy and I just listened to the radio and sat in awe looking at the majestic mountains and the Matanuska and Knik Rivers that we could see from our perch. Those two rivers run into Cook Inlet and the tides determine whether the river is big or small.

The "flats" below the bluff were abounding with wild life. We watched bald eagles soar on the currents as they hunted their prey. It was a glorious sight.

Then, we went to a big clearing that was just like somebody's well-manicured lawn in the middle of all the hay. We had taken our blankets out of the car, spread them out and stretched out to watch the eagles hunt.

After a while, we decided that we were getting awfully warm, so we took our clothes off and stretched out for a good sun bath. We could still hear Dave going around and around while he was cutting the hay and coming closer to what we thought was our private spot. We could smell the sweet-smelling fragrance of new-mown hay.

We stood up to rearrange our blankets, and then heard Dave laughing at us. We looked around and saw him pointing at another hill. Since he was always full of fun, I told Cindy that "he just wants us to think that someone's here", so we ignored him. Every time he passed us, he was laughing harder. I'm sure that he had happy tears in his eyes, as he was laughing so hard.

Too soon, the hay was down and drying fast in all the heat from the sun beating down. Dave shut off the tractor and grabbed the cooler from the truck and came to join us girls. A big, mischievous grin lit up his happy face as he came to where we were soaking up the sun.

When he got there, he laughed until he cried. When he could finally talk, he told us that someone had a transit set up on the other hill and hadn't moved once while we were having our sun bath. Apparently a surveyor was enjoying the show in the middle of the hay field! It didn't take Cindy and I long to jump into our clothes then! We ate our lunch, and then Cindy got onto the old dump rake and started getting the hay into pitchable piles.

What a grand day we had! Thank you, God for that fun, glorious day!

The next day, we went to load the dry, sweet smelling hay onto the trailer and take it home. When we got there, the horses were sticking their noses over the fence while they watched us unload the hay near their pen. We didn't know yet that there were so few of those days left to our family.

We had a family tradition that each August, Dave our boys and his closest friends all went moose hunting together. We had to do some work on the hunting rig to get it ready for the fall hunt. The men and boys would leave early the next morning for their moose hunt. Groceries were loaded onto the hunting rig and final preparations were made.

The hunting party was excited about their upcoming hunt and with happy anticipation they made their final plans for their yearly adventure. Glenn, who was eighteen, had been going on the hunt every year since he was thirteen, but Rick could hardly wait to go on his first hunting trip with his Dad and the other hunters. Cindy was sixteen and couldn't have cared less about hunting.

Chapter 24

On that hunt in 1973, our family's world turned upside down.

When the time came, the hunting gear and supplies were loaded. The track rig was put on the trailer and off they went--happy as could be to be on their annual adventure in the wilderness. They, of course, had no idea of the horrors, which were ahead.

Two days later, Dave and Rick had come home in the middle of the night because Rick had dumped some gas on the campfire (a big no-no) and had caught his shirt on fire. He had a deep burn on a little spot on his stomach. We had called Doc, our friend and neighbor, to come over and check Rick's burn. He cleaned it up, and told us that even though it wasn't very big, it was a bad burn. He assured us that with care it would be fine.

It had rained the whole hunting trip, but the next morning was beautiful and sunny. Dave wanted to let the other hunters know that Rick was O.K. Doc had an airplane, so they made plans for Doc to fly to them to the hunting camp and drop a note to the hunting party. That way, they would continue with their hunt and not worry about Rick. Also, he wanted to let them know that the weather forecast was for more sunny weather.

I had planned to go the Alaska State Fair with friends, so when they asked me to go with them on the plane ride, I turned them down. But, they finally talked me into going. I told them I had to change my shoes, so I took off my clogs and put on my cotton tennis shoes, without socks. I told Dave and Doc that I took the clogs off because, at least if we crashed, the tennis shoes wouldn't fly off and kill someone!

We then got to the airport and the plane wouldn't start. I still didn't want to go, so I told them I would go back home, and come to pick them up when they got back and buzzed the house. They insisted that I go, and that all they had to do to get the plane started was to jump the battery. Dave wanted me to sit up front so that I could see really well. Since I was a lot smaller than Dave was, I told him I would sit in the back and would be able to see just fine from there.

Eventually, they got the plane started and we were off into the blue, blue sky. Along the way, Doc flew low so that we could see the bears eating berries off the hillsides. We soon spotted our hunting party. It was about 70 miles north of Anchorage on a plateau near the area known as Petersville.

Doc was showing Dave how slow the Beechcraft would fly, so he dropped the flaps and lowered the landing gear. Since my uncle was a flying instructor, he had taught my brother and me how to fly when I was 16 and I knew to sit up and look at the gauges. In a plane like that, 85 mph is stall speed and the gauge was showing 85 mph. I told Doc to get the plane up, just as he threw the note out.

I heard Doc say, in a calm voice "Oh, my God!" That was all. The plane had hit a small spruce tree and a wing had been torn off the left side of the plane. There was fire and the plane hit the tops of four small swamp spruce, and, like a boomerang, it was flipped upside down onto it's top. There was an explosion and the fire was to the right of me. I heard Dave say, "My God, somebody help me, Phyllis is back there!" I told him to undo his seat belt and get out of there.

It took me a few seconds to release my seat belt and the next thing I knew I was on my back by the burning wing. The window of the plane was too small for me to go through, but somehow I had gone through it. My left foot was caught and I couldn't get away. I kept working at it, and soon broke free. I believe that God and his angels got me out of that plane and away from that burning plane.

I rolled on the grass and used my hands to put out the fire in my hair. By now, Glenn, who saw it all happen, was trying to get to the plane to help his Dad and Doc. I told Glenn that if they weren't out, they were gone. My heart was broken. Sometimes my heart still bleeds.

Glenn helped me to a nearby creek. He was afraid that I was going to die too, but I told him that there was no way that I was going to die, because I wasn't even hurt! I got into the creek and used my hands to splash water onto my head and face. I saw the skin falling off my hands so I knew then that they were badly burned.

By then, the rest of the hunting party (our good friends Russell, Lance Campbell and Coker, and my brother-in-law,

Loren Dodds) were there doing what they could to help get me out of the creek. While they were trying to help me, I saw the most beautiful white cloud with a glittering gold spiral staircase. It had to be the stairway to heaven. I think that Dave and Doc must have used it, but I couldn't leave the kids yet. It was all so final. So over and done with. I really can't explain the feeling. Dave was gone and in heaven and I had to finish raising my three loving children with God's help.

The hunters were trying their best to get me out of the creek and I didn't want to get out. God was telling me to stay in the creek. When they finally got me out of the creek, I told the hunters to cut my clothes off. I had had on a nylon sweater and jeans that were part nylon. The sweater was melted and mostly gone, but the jeans were just hard and brittle. My nylon bra had melted, but my cotton underpants and cotton shoes did not. My feet and buttocks were the only parts of my body, which didn't suffer burns.

Then hunters told me they had no scissors. I told them to use their hunting knives and to cut off ALL my clothes--there was no modesty left to worry about, so they did. Then I told them to put me into a sleeping bag. They dug out their clean T-shirts and lined the sleeping bag. My face and body just looked red at this time, but my hands were obviously badly burned.

Another small airplane had seen us crash and had called a chopper from Talkeetna, about 25 air miles away. The chopper pilot said that I would never make it sitting up in a small helicopter, so he radioed Elmendorf Air Force Base, near Anchorage, for the medivac unit.

I don't have any idea how much time passed before we heard the big chopper. I do know that the fire from the crash was out so the hunters started another big, smoky, fire to guide them in. The medivac unit spotted us and landed nearby.

It wasn't long before the medics put me onto a stretcher and tried to get an IV started after poking, poking and poking me to no avail. I finally told them to just take me to the hospital. Glenn and Loren went with me. By now, I just was getting sicker and sicker and was soon throwing up. The medics were really worried about my condition as I was in shock.

It was about 3:00 p.m. (about three hours after the crash) before we got to Providence Hospital in Anchorage. The next thing I knew was that a doctor was whacking off my hair and telling a nurse to cut off my rings. She couldn't get the rings off, as my fingers were terribly swollen, but the doctor barked at her that he wanted those rings off! The nurse followed his orders and got the rings off, giving me my first taste of the torture which was to come, and which I got very familiar with over the next few months.

The doctor wanted to immediately medivac me to a burn unit in Houston, Texas, but there was no way that I was going to Texas and leave my family. My body was critically injured, but I still had the ability to know that I needed to be near my family and they needed to have me nearby.

My parents lived in Soldotna, Alaska, at that time, which was about three hours away by car. They had been notified, and my heart just ached for them.

Crash site with burning airplane   Hunters working on me

Chapter 25

The prognosis was grim. The doctors said that I might live 48 hours, if that long. My lungs were burned and 65% of my body had third degree burns and all the rest, except my feet and buttocks, had second degree burns. The doctors told me that my getting in the creek probably saved my life. It turned out that God had told me what to do and by listening to Him, I had done everything right.

The next thing that I remember was being in an oxygen tent. A male nurse came in to weigh me. He had to get me onto my back and onto a scale. What agony! The scales showed 170 pounds. I told him that his scales must be way off, because I only weighed 125 pounds. He said that the scales were right, and it was a good thing that my body was able to retain the fluid, or I would be dead. At that point, I looked like a big charcoal blob. My family could only recognize me by my voice, and I didn't talk much since moving my mouth was so painful.

That same day, the doctor came in and pulled my right arm out from the moist tent, took a scalpel, and sliced the top of my hand three times and twice above the wrist. Such pain! Boy, did I ever hate that doctor for awhile! I found at that the doctor was Dr. Robert Mallin, who had just come to Anchorage from Chicago the week before and he was preparing to be a plastic and restorative surgeon. It turned out that he used me as his patient to become Board certified.

I soon learned that he had put the slits in my hand and arm to keep the circulation going while they tried to save my hand. I had already lived more than 48 hours, beating the odds, and they must have decided to start trying to save different sections of me.

Waiting for help   Glenn Dilley with Air Force Rescue Crew

Chapter 26

While I lay semiconscious in my paper-lined hospital bed in my paper tent, my swollen, black, bloated body, bare of any clothes touching me, arrangements were being made for a double funeral service for my beloved mate and Doc.

Although my body was already enduring more pain than I had ever imagined, the additional agony of mind and heart was almost more than I could bear. Only my faith in God, and my knowledge (through the Bible) that I would see Dave again in a glorious after life, made living and breathing bearable.

My lover, my best friend, and the loving father of my kids was no longer here for us to lean on like we always had. I had to be strong, and with God's help, I was like a rock.
I had promised Glenn at the crash site that I had no intention of dying, and now I really had to follow through on that promise, and with the prayers of my friends and family, as well as my own, I was able to do just that.

My precious, loving Mom stayed with me during the funeral service. I can hardly remember it, but I'm sure that she did. My Dad and Loren and Betty (God bless them) were doing their best to comfort my children through the ordeal.

That day was the second worst of my life. During my conscious moments I could sense Mom's tears as they gently rolled down her beautiful soft cheeks. She couldn't even hold my hand or touch me in any way to comfort me, as I was used to being comforted and touched.

Dave had always been very affectionate and loving to me. Now that was gone from this life forever.

I also had a secret. The coroner had said that Dave had died instantly. Therefore, everyone took comfort that he hadn't realized what had happened to him. But, I knew better. I had decided that I would never tell anyone that Dave's last words had been "Somebody help me, Phyllis is back there". I became aware that I had to undo my seatbelt and get out of the inferno. That was when I had told him to undo his seatbelt and get out of there. But, he couldn't.

After the funeral service was over, many of our family and friends went to our house to reminisce about Dave and Doc. While they were at our house, there was a small earthquake. Eleanor, who was one of my neighbors and a best friend, remembers that earthquake very well. She has recalled that although there was do damage and it wasn't a 'big one', everyone in the house understood it to be a sign of the power of God.

Chapter 28

After five days, the doctors had to set up a special room for me, because at that time, there was no burn unit at Providence Hospital. The room had to be kept at 90 degrees. The bed had paper sheets and I lay in a tent so the paper wouldn't stick to my body. Fluid and blood just oozed out of all parts of my body. I couldn't feed myself and, as you might imagine, using the bedpan was unbearable. You can't imagine what agony it was to use the bedpan after they had taken new skin from my buttocks for grafts.

As time went on, they started taking me to the whirlpool bath--the REAL torture chamber! They gave me medication, but it did nothing to help the pain. They had to slide me onto a rubber sling, then get me into the bubbling water, which was kept at 90 degrees. Then, two doctors and two therapists started to work on me with their scrapers, knives and pliers; scrubbing, rubbing, scraping and tearing off my skin. At that point, they had decided that my face had "only" second degree burns and that I wouldn't need skin grafts. I was relieved at that news.

When they had finished getting off all the dead skin and flesh that they could for the day, they lifted the sling out of the water. Talk about the fires of hell! When the air hits that bare flesh without the protection of skin, hell is the only way to describe it. They would quickly smear a salve and

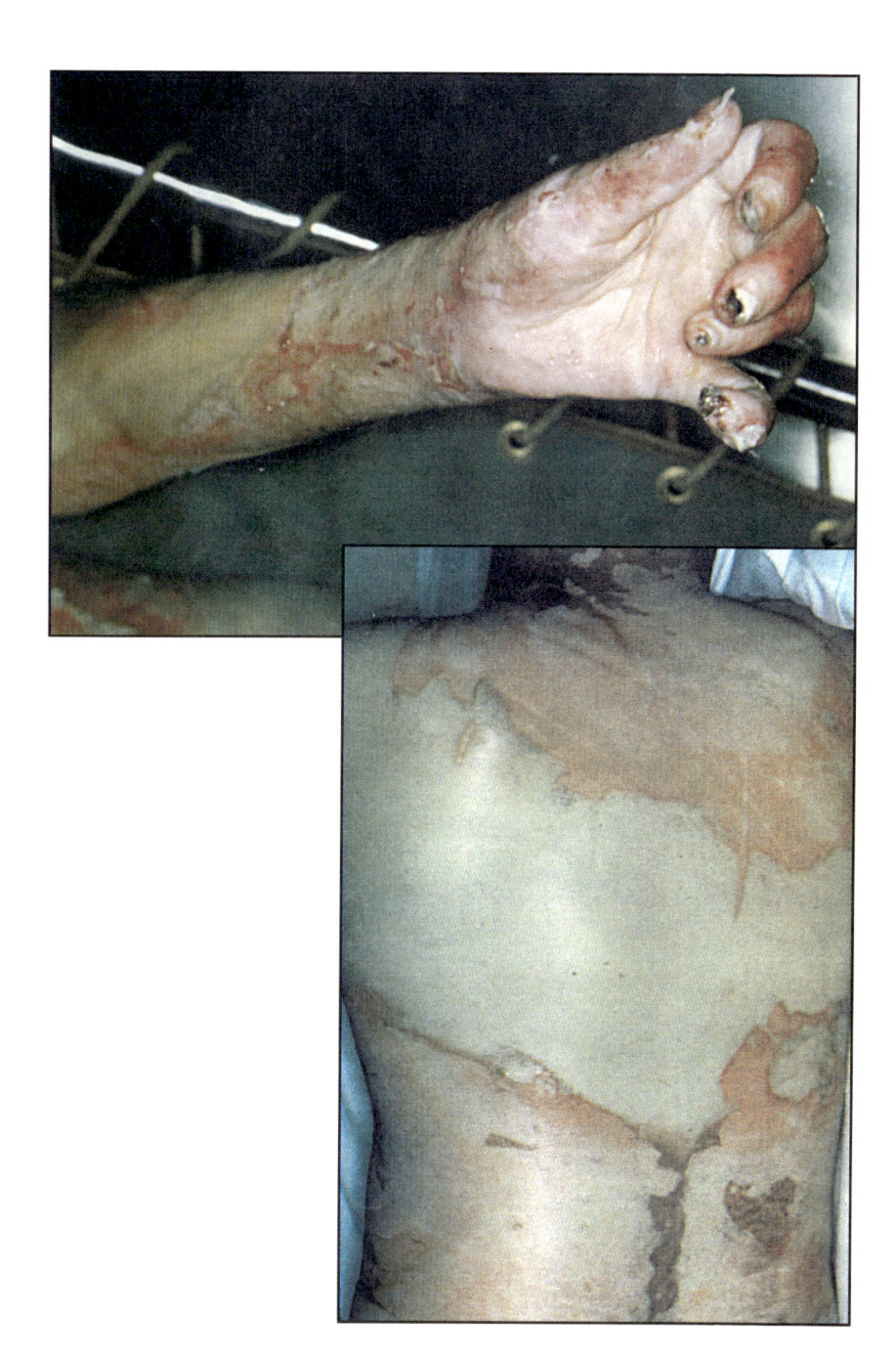

Sling removing me from whirlpool

Back in process of healing (after one month)

place some pigskin on the exposed flesh. That covering made the pain bearable.

When I got back to my room, the old tough, ex-Marine nurse had my bed all ready. Heat pads and about twenty little pillows are ready and she was waiting to tuck me in. She was as tough as they come, but always so kind to me. All the nurses were as kind as their tasks allowed them to be, but she was special. Even when she was off duty, she came back to spoon feed me a milk shake. That took a long time because my mouth would hardly open and I really didn't want to eat.

Chapter 29

One sunny, beautiful day, Mom and Dad had driven up from Soldotna to spend the weekend with the kids and to visit and encourage me. I had not been doing very well. I had a infection and was really down in the dumps. The doctors were concerned about me, because up until then I had done so well.

One of the wonderful nurses had put me in a wheelchair so I could go to the hall window to look at the beautiful day outside that hospital which had become a nightmare to me. As I looked out of the window, I could see the mountain that we call "Sleeping Lady" and the golden sun shining on the top of the mountain. The sun was making the water in Cook Inlet practically glow. I could also see the bustling people going by in their cars, going about their business and being happy.

Then, I heard the sound of the elevator as the therapist came for me with an empty wheelchair. After he found my bed with bloody sheets, but with me not there, he came looking for me to go to the whirlpool and more pain. Looking out the window and seeing the outside world was the most pleasant time that I had had in a long time, and I wasn't ready to give it up for more torture. So, I just told the fine young man that I was taking the day off! I wasn't going with him!

Mom and Dad had been sitting with me and they encouraged me to go on to therapy, and promised to be back in an hour and a half. I knew that if I gave in and went with the therapist that my day would be over. The painkillers would make me sleepy and I wouldn't be able to enjoy the visit of my loving parents.

It didn't take long for the word to get around that I was being obstinate. Soon, the doctors and two whirlpool experts came to talk to us. They explained that I had no choice but to go and let them get the rotten skin and flesh off NOW! They told me to tell my folks good-bye, and they whisked me off to my torture chamber. Mom and Dad did come back, like they promised, but I hardly knew that they were there.

They were able to get rid of the staph infection. Fortunately, it was the "good" kind that was treatable with antibiotics. That was the first and last time that I refused my treatments. But anyone who has been in that situation knows what fear and dread of the torture I was feeling. When people are standing around you picking and tearing your skin and flesh, you get really tired of that process in a hurry!

When it comes to the physical therapy, they let you know in a hurry that if a part of you won't bend, it will bend when they get done with it. Even though you think the ordeal of therapy will kill you, it's only through that process that you can get your motion back in your hands and legs again.

I managed to live through all that with help of God. Others will too, if they have faith. I had to keep reminding myself that God wasn't going to leave me and He wasn't going to give me more than He and I could bear. A body can bear a lot more than you can imagine.

When the doctors came in to take the blood gas tests, the only place he could take it was by cutting down the artery on the inside of my thigh, inside my groin. After more medicine, I could finally sleep for awhile.

When I woke up, my family and friends were there, wearing paper gowns masks slippers and gloves. I noticed that lots of the people, whom I might have expected to come, didn't! No one stayed long. I really couldn't talk much and I'm sure that my room was much too hot for most people. The kids took turns feeding me my supper. What patience and love it must have taken for them to go through that ordeal with me! Eating was so slow for me since I could hardly chew.

Chapter 30

Cindy and Glenn were both working so that they could keep the house going. Boy, it was hard on everyone! There was no insurance on the airplane, so I didn't get one penny. The State of Alaska had passed a law, which had just gone into effect that July that an estate could not be sued more than 90 days after the incident. Because I was in the hospital, in no condition to be filing lawsuits, I wasn't able to meet the deadline. The doctor's widow disappeared outside of Alaska and didn't offer to pay any of my expenses.

A few days after my first whirlpool experience, I had my first skin grafts. All the skin for grafting had to come from my buttocks, as that was the only unburned area I had. They stretched that skin so that it would cover more area, and when they did that, it looked like fish scales. They got as much as they could from me, but still had to use pigskin while I grew more that could be grafted to cover the bare flesh.

About two weeks after the first whirlpool bath, I heard the doctor talking to the orthopedic surgeon outside my door. My doctor was saying that they would have to take my right arm and right foot off. The ankle of my right foot was just black bone and strings of black nerves and muscle. My right hand and arm had so much nerve damage that they believed it would never work. But, the orthopedic surgeon said that he would like to try to save them first. Everything

was rigid. Even though nothing would bend, you'd better believe that the therapists could make them move--the doctors and therapists told me that I was a very classy cusser. I knew then, and I know now, that it was only through help of God that I was able to endure the pain.

Chapter 31

One day, at the whirlpool, the doctor threw in a rubber duck and asked me if I could snorkel. Even though they had thought that my face had had second degree burns, they had decided that the right side had third degree, and was dead and rotting, and that they had to debride it while I snorkeled. My right ear was rotting, so it would also be gone.

No one in the world should have to snorkel while his or her skin and flesh is being ripped off. Now, the right side of my face and my neck would need skin grafts, and the ear would have to be reconstructed.

The doctors told me to drink at least six beers a day to help keep my kidneys and bladder working. I have never liked beer, and if I drank at all, I would have preferred a margarita. I told them so, and they just laughed at me. So, I had a refrigerator full of beer. As it turned out, they had moved another bed into my room and my new roommate, a 25-year-old man, who just had burned hands, really liked my supply of beer. It worked out O.K., because people kept bringing me beer, and I could only get down two a day and his help freed up room in the refrigerator for the new donations.

My new roommate was burned in some type of explosion. It was good to have someone to visit with to help pass the time, if we were both awake at the same time.

By that time, I had progressed far enough along that my ankle was good enough to walk on, so the therapists decided it was time to try to walk. When they stood me up, the blood ran from everywhere into pools around my feet. This didn't stop their determination that I should walk, so we proceeded with the therapy. I left a bloody trail down the hospital hallway as I went.

My Marine nurse was still taking extra special care of me, keeping heating pads and pillows in my bed for my return from the torture chambers. She also massaged my feet, which was the only pleasant feelings I had at that point in my recovery. My feet were the only place on me that could be massaged.

At that point, I had been in the hospital about a month. I had progressed well enough that the orthopedic doctor wanted to show off to everyone how well I could flex my foot. It worked great. He was thrilled and so was I--it worked as well as ever! (In looking back, I wonder what my doctor would think if he knew that since then I have worked more or less constantly for over the past ten years, nearly every day as a cook at the local senior citizens center, standing on my feet, and using my right hand to mix and stir and lift heavy loads! And, before I took that job, I had gone back to work cooking at Dimond High School, preparing food for over 3,500 students per day! I believe that it was a miracle, which was done by God through that surgeon that gave me back the ability to make a living for my family.)

Every day was the same routine--whirlpool, pigskin, therapy and more walking. Every day was better, with less bleeding. The grafts were tightening up. My chest and stomach felt like saddle leather, and it was so tight that it was hard to breathe. My neck was pulling my head down and to the right. They knew that they would have to do surgery to release the tightness, and would have to do still more skin grafts.

By then, I could not have any anesthesia because I had built up immunity, and if they gave me enough to put me under, it could kill me. They did try to give me shots for the pain, but they didn't last long enough for the doctors to do their work. In spite of this, the doctors had to proceed with the repairs I needed. I did a lot of praying for more strength during those procedures.

My right eye wouldn't close, so they had to take some of the eyelid from my left eye and put it in the right eyelid. I had to have a new right ear made out of plastic tubing and skin. They had wanted to build a complete new ear, but enough was enough, and I drew the line at just enough to hold my glasses on.

I recently obtained and read my medical records, as well as I could understand the medical language! The orthopedic doctor who fixed my hands and ankle had to replace all the cartilage in my hands and right ankle because it had been completely destroyed. The medical records indicated that I should be eligible for disability the rest of my life since I had lost 60% of the use of my hands. However, I can do just about anything I want to do. Picking up buttons, needles and other small items is hard to do, but I do them anyway. In fact, I like to come up with things to do that makes me use my hands as much as possible.

Chapter 32

As soon as I was able to get up and walk, I asked the nurses if I could visit the lady across the hall from my room. Every night she called continuously for her baby. It broke my heart and I wanted to reach out to her. I thought her baby had died. But, the nurse told me that the lady (Doris) had hit a moose near the Army base and, although her body showed no signs of damage, her brain had been destroyed. The nurse said that, as far as they knew, she had had no baby. I decided to go see her anyway, so, with the help of the nurses, I hobbled into her room. I was in excruciating pain, and my legs bled profusely from the fresh skin grafts.

The nurse opened the door to her room, and there on the pillow lay the most beautiful face and long red hair spread out across that hospital-white pillow.

That was the moment that I decided that I was really lucky. Even though I had been severely injured, and even had some brain damage, I had the ability to think and recognize my family and get ready to go on with my life. I stood there in a pool of blood around my feet and thanked God that He had spared me.

It wasn't long before Doris' parents came from Arkansas to take her back with them to care for her the rest of her life. They certainly had a heavy cross to bear and I only hoped that they would be able to cope with the burden.

I remembered the Bible lesson about contentment and that we are supposed to be content no matter what the situation. God had let me live and for that I was very contented. He won't ever give us more of a load than we can bear and for this I thanked Him. I knew that I would go home to a nice house and a loving family and lots of supportive friends. I would get to be with my three wonderful children as they grew into adulthood, and for that I was contented. I knew that my parents and Dave's sister and brother-in-law would not let us go hungry, and for that I was contented. In fact, after I saw Doris, I spent a lot of time counting my blessings.

Chapter 33

The doctors had decided that if I had someone stay with me at all times that I could go home in time for Thanksgiving. I still had some open wounds. The doctors even went to my house to talk to my kids and to see if it was clean and pleasant. Because most patients in my condition turned to drugs or alcohol, the environment I would be in at home was important to them.

They told the kids that our old dog would have to go. Old Duke was deaf and slept on the couch. He wet the bed at night. I had a rubber sheet and a quilt I used just for him. We washed his quilt every day, but that wasn't good enough for the doctors. So, the veterinarian went to the house and put Old Duke to sleep, on his favorite place, the couch. I had always been the one to carry him into the veterinarian's office, and they knew that since I couldn't do that this time, he would have been afraid, so they came to him.

At that point, I was still in the hospital while the kids got things ready for me to go home. Cindy knew how I felt about animals and how the loss of Old Duke would upset me.

One day, she showed up at the hospital with her parka on. When she opened her coat, a little boxer puppy was snuggled against her. She put him on my bed just as a nurse walked in. The nurse's mouth fell open, and then she said, "I'm going to pretend that I didn't see that!"

The new puppy, which we named "Nick" was very cute, but he turned out to be quite retarded. When he was home alone he destroyed everything that he could get to. We thought that he would outgrow that phase, thinking that he was just a puppy. But, it didn't take too long for us to figure out that he wasn't going to change. So, our neighbor took him to the dog pound for us. They hadn't even gotten to the door when some people came in and adopted him.

Like us, they thought he was cute, but we learned later that they had to have him put to sleep after just a couple of weeks because he was destructive in their home, too. I'm sure that Nick could have used some medication to calm him down.

One of Cindy's friends, Melody, stayed with our family so Glenn and Cindy could work. Melody worked the opposite shift, so between the three of them and Rick, I would never be alone.

I had to agree to arrange a ride to therapy every day. At that point, I was afraid of everything--riding in a car or even walking across the room. So, the ride to therapy had to be very slow and they had to be very gentle with me, and they were--God bless them!

Chapter 34

Just because I was home, I didn't stop the treatments. I had to have a bath in musk oil three times a day followed by a rub down all over my body with Vaseline (it's too bad I didn't own stock in the company that made Vaseline!). Next, they had to wrap me totally, but very carefully, with elastic bandages. They had to be careful that my circulation wasn't cut off anywhere. Every session was the "not so loose, not so tight, and absolutely no wrinkles" routine.

I was as stiff as a board, so it took three of them just to get me into the tub. Every morning, my right arm was clinched tight against my chest with bent elbow.

I worked to straighten it all day long, in agony, and by bedtime, it would be straight. But, the next morning, it was the same all over again. This went on for months, until it finally stayed straight.

I had kept the secret about Dave's last words until about a month after I had been home. But, one night as the kids were going through the rubdown routine, I was sobbing my heart out. The kids knew that something was dreadfully wrong, so I had to finally tell them the truth. We hugged and cried for hours that night. I believe that that big release allowed me to get over the worst of my grief. I was finally able to cope with the reality. Even so, it's O.K. to cry, and I still do when something brings up an old memory.

God and His angels must have been guiding my children. Even at this time in their lives when most children are interested in their friends and doing the things teenagers do, my well being and treatments were the only concerns my three children had for months and months.

Cindy had a list on the refrigerator outlining all the regular chores. She rotated the chore duties regularly, so that each had a turn doing something different. Because of Dr. Mallin's orders, the house had to be kept exceptionally clean for me. They all worked very hard to keep it spotless and sanitized. You must remember that Glenn and Cindy were both working and Rick was in school during this time. It was a heavy load to bear, but they bore up very well, with God's help.

I hope that they know and understand how loved that they are. Not only for all they did for me, but also as the parents they now are to my grandchildren and the people they are in their workplaces. The trauma of losing their father so tragically and going through my ordeal with me could have deeply damaged them, but it seemed to strengthen them, just as it did for me.

Chapter 35

During that time period, I had to go back into the hospital for surgery many times. My neck was so tight on my right side that it pulled my head over and I couldn't straighten my head upright. My right eye still wouldn't close all the way. I had to wear a big Band-Aid over my eye every night so that it wouldn't dry out.

At one point, an eye specialist fitted me with a contact lens for my right eye, with the idea that it would help keep the eye moist and take care of the scars on it. So, I went home with the new contact lens in my eye. But, there was a complication--I had had to have pins placed in all my fingers to try to keep them from curling as they healed and the pins each stuck about one-quarter inch out from the tip of my fingers.

My instructions were to take the contact out at night and put the Band-Aid on my eye, as I had been doing. About 11:00 p.m. the first night I was home with the contact lens, I remembered that this chore needed to be done. I took one look at my hands and knew that I wouldn't be able to do the job, so each of the kids tried to get the contact lens out of my eye, to no avail. So, we got a neighbor to come over to do the job. After trying and trying, she finally got it out, and promptly threw the lens in the trash! I don't know which of us wasn't thinking so well when the plan was made, the eye specialist or me!

My right eye still has scars on it, but I can see pretty well out of it. I remember that the doctor always made early morning appointments for me, to save me embarrassment.

Chapter 36

One time when I was in the hospital for more neck grafts and was on the operating table when the plastic surgeon got called out on a great emergency! So, they just bandaged me up and went to take care of the desperate man. I learned later that a grizzly bear had met the man on the trail and had slapped him in the face, taking his face off to the point that it was only hanging by a very small strip of skin.

He recovered, but had a big cross to bear. I never did get to meet that man, but I often think about him.

They had taken me back to my room during the time that the surgeon was taking care of that emergency. At one time, I kind of woke up and there was lots of blood all over my pillow. The unfinished skin graft had broken loose! About that time, Rick came to see me. I saw him standing at the foot of my bed turning white. He started to fall backward, stiff as a board. Even though I was groggy and still stiff, I was fast! I flew out of that bed and grabbed his shirt, letting him down gently, so that he wouldn't bump his head when he fell. I forgot at the time that I had on my "backless, topless, bottomless" hospital gown. The three other people in the room must have had a good show of my bare rear end! I guess this little episode shows that the instincts of a mother to protect her child from hurt outweigh modesty!

The nurse came with smelling salts to revive Rick. By then, there was blood everywhere, so the nurse had to put compresses and pressure on my open wound for hours, until the surgeon could come back to finish his job. I often wonder how my children did as well as they did when they visited me during those long months when I looked so horrible.

I had to go back and get my neck worked on again just a few years ago. It was finally almost comfortable, after twenty years.

Chapter 37

After I went home, I never went anywhere except therapy. I looked like a real monster. A week before Christmas, Mom came and wanted me to take her Christmas shopping. I told her that Cindy could do it when she got home, but Mom told me, "no way, we're going shopping like we used to". Anyway, she won.

We lived on the outskirts of Anchorage, and she wanted to go downtown to Penney's. I still didn't like to ride in cars, and this was my first time to drive since the accident. We got to the parking garage, and I parked the car. Then, I told Mom that I would wait in the car. So, she just sat there, too. Then she told me that I hadn't gone through everything I had gone through to live like a hermit. She told me, "You're alive. Now quit feeling sorry for yourself. You're still you. So, let's go have fun!" We had a big hug and lots of tears, and then we started laughing.

So, I got my leathery, scarred, body out of the car, into the world and back into life. There were lots of people shopping, as you could imagine at Christmas-time. Everyone looked at me. Some stared. Little kids would say, "Mommy, look at that lady's face" (Thank God they couldn't see the rest of my body!) Every time that happened, I told them that I had been in a plane crash and now you can see what fire can do to you. I also told them to never play with fire.

When we went to lunch I told the waitress that we were celebrating my new life after tragedy. She was very pleasant and we talked a little about my situation.

Chapter 38

My next major step came that same December when I got on an AIRPLANE and flew to Hawaii with my parents and Rick. Mom had called to tell me that she and Dad were going to Hawaii just before Christmas and that they had tickets for Rick and me to go with them.

I wasn't sure then that I ever intended to ever get into another airplane for any reason, but the kids begged for me to go. After all, the reservations were all in place and it would have been a shame for me to mess things up! After all, school would be out for the holidays, so I would only miss a few days of work.

So, the next morning, I called Dr. Mallin for some tranquilizers to enable me to handle it. He gave his blessings for the trip, but warned me to buy a big hat and to be careful not to get much sun on any part of my body. He lectured me that I didn't need tranquilizers. After all, I'd gotten that far on sheer will power, faith and persistence and that I would do just fine without medication. I accepted what he said, but when that big plane took off, I couldn't breathe for awhile. Talk about white knuckles! But, I didn't scream, and not screaming had been my goal.

The flight was uneventful. The landing was very difficult for me, but I put it behind me once we got our things together and headed for the beauty and wonderful smell of the islands.

The flowers were so fragrant. It was glorious. I thanked God for the beauty of Hawaii and for letting me go on such a wonderful vacation. I thanked Him that I had come so far in just a year. The previous December I was barely home from the hospital and now, just a year later, I was experiencing such beauty with my family!

We saw and did everything that we could think of and find time for. I particularly enjoyed my trip to Maui.

When we had gotten to Maui, Rick and I had to share a king size bed in one room. The clerk was upset when she saw us, but since there were no other rooms, she let us have the room. We managed just fine.

Rick made friends with the local children and really enjoyed himself playing on the beach with them. Mom, Dad and I could sit at the outdoor cafe and watch them play in the ocean. We also enjoyed watching the birds flying all around the crawly creatures and us as they moved around.

In the evening we enjoyed relaxing some more and taking in all that we could absorb of God's glorious sunset.

I had such a great time that I was actually relaxed on the plane ride back to Alaska!

When we got back to our house, we walked into a Christmas card with the fireplace going, the Christmas tree up and candy for the kids.

In just two short days it would be Jesus' birthday and we would celebrate by opening our own beautifully wrapped gifts. What peace, love, and joy we shared!

Chapter 39

My second cousin, Chet Barker's, wife Doris and her son, Dale, came to Alaska for a three-month visit, and to help out, in February 1974. Doris and her husband, Chet, have always been close to our family, and had been to visit us in Alaska before.

Although the kids never said anything, I'm sure that they were relieved to have some of the heavy load taken off their young shoulders.

Russell had moved into our trailer house as soon as we had moved out, in December 1972. Russell wasn't home much, as he worked on the oil fields of the North Slope, and had since 1969, but it was nice to have him in the trailer when he was home. Since he didn't use the trailer full time, Doris and Dale stayed in there when Russell was gone and stayed in the house with us when he was home.

Dale started school with Rick and everyone had settled in nicely. Although we had some really good visits, I still was only going outside the house to therapy.

Of course, some people were curious about my scars, but by then, they had become a part of me and I hardly ever pay attention to them. If strangers obviously notice them, I just tell them how I was hurt.

Chapter 40

Russell's daughter, Tammy, came to stay with him during the summer of 1974 and planned to go to school in Alaska that fall. Tammy and Cindy were about the same age and instantly became best friends. They really enjoyed themselves together. They decided that they should make their fortunes by going to work in the fish cannery at Naknek, on Bristol Bay, as soon as school was out. Naknek is a small Alaskan Native settlement, which had very few conveniences available for the cannery workers.

So, the girls set up a tent, fixed themselves a stove and laid out their bedrolls. They didn't realize that they were camped right next to the local dump and that there were lots of bears, which considered the dump to be their private cafe. But, it didn't take them long to decide that they had better relocate their campsite!

They did get work at the cannery and their first job was "sliming" fish--washing the slime off the fish and pulling out the entrails. That was not the fortune-making dream job that they had come for! A short time later, Cindy had gone out on a fishing boat as a cook. At least there were no bears on the boat and she had a real bunk! Tammy went to work at the only restaurant in Naknek, which was an absolute zoo during the salmon season. She still keeps in touch with the lady who owned that restaurant.

Both girls did make good money that summer, and while they were doing it, they had the adventures of a lifetime. The two of them became like blood sisters, and are still close to this day.

Chapter 41

I had improved enough over the summer that work the fall of 1974, just a year after the accident I decided to go back to work at Dimond High School when school started in the fall. I have never been one to sit around and I was going bananas. After all, I thought I had improved enough to clean the house, so I could go back to work.

The doctors hadn't wanted me to go back to work cooking at Dimond High School because they thought the kids would be cruel. But I found that the kids were all super and kind to me. Of course, most of them knew my story as my children went to school with them.

Although I was getting a Social Security check for disability, I definitely preferred working. With the help of my boss, Eva Reese, I started with just 3 hours a day. Boy, was I ever weak and tired after that short time--my legs throbbed and my hands ached.

After a month of working part time, I went back on a full schedule. The hard physical work helped me gain my strength back.

At that time, we were preparing meals for an average of three thousand students every day--all those at Dimond High School, plus six other schools that we sent lunch out on mobile units. Not only did my helper, Yvonne Emery, and I prepare all the food (from scratch), we had to pack and load the mobile units. Yvonne was a really hard worker and we worked as a team. I still don't understand how we managed to do all that every day! But, the kids loved the food and I love feeding good food to people, so I was happy, even if I was tired.

After I had worked a few months, Social Security sent me a letter telling me that I had to repay three months of my disability check. I protested the decision and went before an appeals judge who told them that anyone in my condition who was even trying to work should never had gotten such a letter. She told me that I could have stayed on disability for the rest of my life, if I had chosen to. She was really upset that I had gotten that letter, because the rules said a person could have a three month trial period to see if they could go back to work, without being penalized.

It felt good to know that if I couldn't keep working, that I wouldn't be without income, but I don't like not being productive and busy.

Chapter 42

I wanted to go to my 20th high school class reunion at Belle Fouche, South Dakota, but I had really mixed feelings about this. My ear surgery hadn't healed up yet and I didn't look anything like I had before. Actually, I looked awful and couldn't even wear any kind of makeup to try to improve things.

I finally did decide to go. Russell was going to his family reunion in Mobridge and Cindy would go along, so I wouldn't be alone on the trip. Our flight was what we call the "red-eye" (leaves Anchorage about 1:00 a.m.) and most people sleep, but I didn't, even though the flight was nice and smooth.

After I was there, I almost chickened out of going to the picnic with all my classmates and their husbands. Cindy took me to the park anyway. All my fears were unfounded. My classmates were so glad to see me and there were hugs all around. Of course, I had to tell them the whole story.

Bobby Gilbert, the "little person" who had been our class king, came right over to claim his queen. We were still the class favorites. I had a wonderful time. That gesture emphasized that my real friends loved me for my inside, not my outside.

On the Monday following the picnic, Cindy and I went to where they raised Chinese pug dogs. We bought a female so that we could have some pups with McDonald, Dave's pug.

Russell came back from his family reunion and took me all around to see my relatives. Cindy and Tammy were having their own reunion, doing what teenagers do.

When it was time to come home, I checked Tisha, the dog, all the way through to Anchorage, so that she could ride with us in the cabin of the plane.

Since there wasn't enough room under the seat of the smaller plane we had to take from Rapid City, South Dakota to Denver, she had to ride in the cargo hold to Denver. That plane didn't fly so high, so she was fine there, but we didn't want her in cargo for the long flight on to Seattle, then Anchorage.

We picked Tisha up at the baggage claim area and had to run to connect with our flight to Seattle. When we got to the plane, they were trying to get the door closed. Russell and the stewardess got into a bit of a tug-of-war over the door-- the stewardess would shut it and Russell would open it! Anyway, we got on.

Cindy put the Tisha's box under her seat and it didn't seem like long before we were landing in Seattle. Our flight crew switched in Seattle. We didn't even get off the plane. While we were waiting for the plane to be serviced and to take off again, Cindy took Tisha out of the box and put her on her lap to pet her and talk to her for awhile.

The other people on the plane were "oohing and aahing" over the cute dog, when the
new stewardess came on board and told us that we would have to put the dog in cargo. You'd better believe that all the passengers exploded! Some of them had a drink or two too many and even went so far as to tell her that if the dog had to ride in cargo, they were getting off too!

It wasn't long before the manager came on board. He took one look at the dog and informed the stewardess that she should have known that pugs can't ride in cargo--their "smashed up" nose won't let them breathe in cargo. Anyway, Tisha rode the rest of the way in the cabin with us and never made a sound. If Cindy hadn't taken her out to pet her, they would never have known she was even there. But, when we got home, Russell let us know that that was his last trip with two women and a dog to look after!

Unfortunately, we never did get any puppies from Tisha and McDonald. But they became best buddies and were really cute together.

Chapter 43

The first summer after the accident, Olive Shelldorf came to visit from Wyoming. While she was here, we decided to experiment with a "new and improved makeup" that was supposed to hide scars and wrinkles.

Olive had spent most of her life outside in the hot, Wyoming, sun and her face was like a road map of gullies. I obviously had scars. So, we got some of the "wonder makeup" and smeared lots of it onto both our faces, probably about 1/8 inch thick--after all, since we each had so many flaws to fill, if a little is good, a lot had to be better.

We both looked like we had been molded in porcelain. We tried to laugh at each other, but couldn't because the makeup had set up so solid that we couldn't move our laugh muscles! It's a good thing that a remover came with it, or we would have been in deep trouble for sure. Between us we used the entire jar of remover, but finally got it off.

Needless to say, we never tried that product again. I suppose that there is probably a product that will do what that one claimed to do, but I certainly never tried any more.
I had sent away for this "miracle" makeup, which I'm sure probably worked for minor blemishes, but not for us.

Chapter 44

In August 1974, a year after the plane crash, one of Rick's friends had spent the night. I had fixed some fried chicken for the boys, but Rick's friend said that he had to get home. So, I told him to grab a chicken leg on the way out, but Glenn, Rick and Rick's friend just left without stopping. A few minutes later, Rick called and told me to get down to Dimond Blvd. immediately. I knew that something was very wrong, so I obeyed. As I pulled out of the garage, I saw Glenn's old sports car, and I knew that the boys had taken Dave's truck.

There was a huge pothole in the road, right on top of the hill. Two young parents who had left their baby girl with their aunt next door were going out to pick up the baby. They had an old Volkswagen Bug and were going too fast. But, instead of going around the pothole on the shoulder, they went around it in the other driving lane.

They hit Glenn and Rick head on and both of the people in the other car were killed instantly. Glenn had a cut on his head but Rick and his friend were just banged up. When the Troopers and medics arrived, they told me to take Glenn to the hospital by way of Kincaid Loop, because Dimond Blvd. was blocked.

Glenn had done nothing wrong, but this tragedy, on top of the witnessing the plane crash that had killed his father and badly burned me, was almost too much for a young man to bear.

That accident took a real toll on everyone. Then, to top it all off, Rick's friend's parents sued us! A doctor had seen both Rick and his friend and, other than bruises and sore muscles, they weren't hurt. But, my insurance company paid them $10,000.00 because they said it was cheaper than going to court.

Many years later, Glenn told me that he had spent a lot of time with a psychiatrist over the combination of events. God bless him.

Chapter 45

While Tammy was going to school and staying with us, Russell came to the house a lot and it wasn't long before we started a big romance! All the kids were really supportive because they already loved him as a "super-uncle" and they knew that he would be good and kind to me and to them.

Russell had worked with Dave in South Dakota and Alaska, so our families had always been in contact. He had been at the plane crash with the hunting party and he knew what he was getting into.

Russell's daughters, Tammy and Shaye, were both thrilled and they were hoping that we would get married. They thought that I'd be the best stepmother ever! Russell wanted to take care of my kids and me, but I still wasn't in any shape to get married.

He was gone for weeks at a time on his job, but when he was home, he usually ate supper with our family. Sometimes we went to the movies or out to dinner (with all the kids). Russell wasn't much for dancing, even though I loved to dance. But, I finally got him to go square dancing with Betty and Loren Dodds, who still lived next door.

I think he actually enjoyed it although, with Russell, it's sometimes hard to tell! We also had a group of friends, who held card parties, so when Russell was home we got together with them and enjoyed playing cards together.

After school started I was busy with my job. The girls from work had always come to my house for a Christmas party and always had such a good time. The kids were busy with their activities. Life went on.

I still had to have some more small operations to fix what they could, even though, in those days, there wasn't a lot that could be done with burns. The Doctor did decide to try sanding some of the scars off my face. It didn't work. Russell thought that I was pretty, scars and all.

One day in the late fall of 1975, we were going to Soldotna to the wedding of some of Russell's friends. Glenn was off work for the weekend, so he went along to see Grandma and Grandpa. The weather was horrendous. There must have been six inches of fresh snow on the road the whole way.

Russ and I were talking about the wedding, and decided to get married, too. I think that he was just worried about my family and wanted to take care of us. Anyway, we got married, just over two years after the plane crash, on October 16, 1975.

Both our entire families were happy. Dave's sister approved and Mom and Dad were thrilled. All our kids were excited to be a "blended" family

Russell and Phyllis Backhaus

Tammy and Shaye Backhaus

Chapter 46

Dad hadn't been feeling well, so he and Mom went back to Hawaii the last part of November 1976. He thought that if he would feel better, out of the cold. After they had only been there for two days, they Mom and said that they were coming home. Dad was real bad. We met them at the airport. I was so shocked when they brought Dad off the plane on a stretcher. He looked so pale that I wanted him to get to the hospital, but he wanted to go to our home. So, that's what we did.

Then, about 2:00 a.m., Mom came to get me and told me that Dad couldn't breathe! We immediately took him to the hospital and they whisked him into the emergency surgery, where they drained fluid from around his heart and lungs. They did a biopsy, then reported to us that the fluid they had drained was malignant. Dad had a very rare and fast kind of cancer.

They had to insert tubes to drain the fluid into jugs by his bed. They also had him on a respirator but took him off after about a week. After they took the respirator off, he could talk and we did a lot of reminiscing. But, he was worried about Christmas.

The doctor said that he could go to my house, if I could take care of him. Of course I could take care of him! But, the next night, I had that awful dream again. This time, there was no doubt that it was my Dad who would die.

Mom and I left early to go to the hospital. For the first time in weeks, he was eating. He had just finished his juice, cream of wheat and toast, and commented that it really tasted good, and wondered if I could get some more for him, so I called the nurse and she ordered a second helping for him.

One minute, he was so happy, and the next minute he had a heart attack. The doctor rushed in and gave him a shot with a long needle, right in his heart. Then, the doctor motioned me out of the room, but Mom stayed with Dad. When the doctor came out of the room, he told me that he thought that Dad would have another heart attack in about two hours, and asked if we wanted him to try to save him again. I said, "no, let him go". I figured that that way would be better than the prolonged hell of cancer.

The doctor was right. In about two hours, God took Dad to heaven. He sat up in bed, and with outstretched arms, said, "I'm going!" I believe that he was reaching out for the hands of God's angels who had come to get him and take him home.

After a few weeks, Mom went to Soldotna to her now lonely home she had shared with my wonderful Dad. She went back to her job, but her health failed immediately, so I made it a point to drive down often to spend time with her. Then, one day a friend of hers called and told us that she had found Mom passed out.

It was then that I took a small plane ride for the first time since the accident. I didn't think I would ever do that again, but I had to get to my mother. The ride was so rough that most of the other people on the plane were sick, but I was so scared that I couldn't get sick.

Mom and I talked it over and decided that she should move in with us, so we loaded her car, rented a trailer, made arrangements to rent her house out, and took her home with me. We found out that her heart was giving her trouble.

Chapter 47

Cindy had met a handsome fellow, who didn't much approve of working, while she was a flagger for a construction company in Fairbanks the year before, and had moved to Minnesota with him after their wedding (that's the one and only time I wore a black dress to a wedding!)

She was working and pregnant. We sent her money for awhile, then I told her that I was sending a plane ticket and for her and her baby, Metis, to come home. She had to sneak away, because the fellow didn't want her out of his sight.

When I went to the airport to pick them up, I hardly recognized Cindy. She was so sick. I took her to an internist the next morning and we found out that she had to have a D&C. She had been living with some afterbirth stuck in her uterus. Metis also needed some loving care, and she had come to the right spot for that!

Metis was the light of our lives and was such a blessing from God. Mom and Metis took care of each other and Mom was so happy. Her health improved, but she was still fragile. Even in her condition, she mopped the floor kitchen floor every night, after everyone else went to bed, so that Metis would have a clean floor to play on.

Mom's lungs would fill with fluid when her heart got too bad. We started giving her oxygen while she slept, and it really helped her. She looked forward every day to going out for a cup of coffee and a little shopping with me when I got home from work.

Cindy was working, so Mom and I took care of Metis. Cindy and Metis had a room at our house, so we all helped each other. Then, Tammy came up again and brought her cat with her. Tammy and Cindy went apartment hunting, but with a cat and a baby, they didn't have any luck.

Russ and I finally bought a mobile home for them to live in. It worked out well for everyone. Cindy took Metis to a babysitter when she went to work. One day, Mom and I picked the baby up on my way home from work. We found her standing at the bottom of the basement steps crying, with her coat still on. Mom and I were very upset at that!

Metis' and Great-Grandma Barker cooking

When Cindy got home from work, Mom instructed her, with wagging finger, to never take Metis' to a baby-sitter again, that between us, we would take care of her at home. I don't think she ever had another baby-sitter except her family.

Metis' was a very good little girl and Grandpa Russell adored her. She is now twenty-one and still a big light in our lives. Thank you, God that you sent us such a wonderful blessing to fill the void left by my wonderful Dad.

Chapter 48

Metis' would be six on her birthday in 1983, and I decided to get her a pony. The pony I found was named "Fiddlestix" and she was half Welsh and half quarter horse. I like that size of horse for myself, too. Fiddlestix was bay in color, with a white star on her forehead, and supposedly well broke.

I decided that I could ride her home, so I put the bridle on her and took off. Russell was going to go to the hardware store for something, so I told him that I would meet him at home, with the horse.

I didn't know anything about this strange horse and I was watching what she would do. She balked at a little stream of water going down a hill into a ditch. I wasn't sure whether she would try to jump it, or balk and refuse to go on. I cinched my legs together, to be ready for a jump, if she decided to do that. I didn't know that she had been trained to go if you squeezed her belly with your legs! So, I ended up on my backside and Fiddlestix headed back to her old home.

I was standing by the highway, waiting for Russell to come back, and wondering how many people going by had seen the show! Russ had a good laugh as he stopped to get me. He teased me " I thought that you could ride a horse". We went back and got her again, and that time, Russell rode her home. That was quite a sight, too. He was riding bareback, right up the highway, and he is so tall, that his feet were practically dragging the ground.

We had built a pole fence around the pasture for her. I went to Anchorage for the weekend because I didn't want Metis' to see her pony until her birthday. I found out later that Fiddlestix had been a show horse and had won the barrel races and pole bending events at the rodeos.

On Metis' birthday, a friend, Teri, who was a good rider, galloped up on Fiddlestix. She got off, bowed, and handed Metis' the reins. Metis' was so tickled. I can't describe how joyous she was!.

Now, I'm a worrywart Grandma, and at that time, Metis' was my only grandchild. She didn't know how to ride, and I had put a long lead line on the horse. For about a month, I was a constant nuisance while she learned. She always complained that I couldn't run fast enough at a trot--she wanted to gallop!

One day, we were at the back of the homestead when she asked if I would please let her go by herself. After a short, silent, prayer, I unsnapped the lead line. Metis' and Fiddlestix spun around and took off at a full run. I was scared that the horse would run away, at least to the barn, which is on the front of the property.

When I got to the house, out of breath, they were nowhere in sight. I really panicked then. But, it wasn't long before they came riding up at a beautiful, slow, lope. Metis' looked, and acted, like she was glued to Fiddlestix. All was well, but

I did lose a lot of good exercise when I let her go on her own.

When Metis' wasn't visiting, either Suzie or I rode Fiddlestix. I put the bareback pad on her because Mr. T, my Boston terrier rode too, I was afraid his toenails would hurt Fiddlestix. (Mr. T. rode the snowmachine and three wheeler, too!)

One fall morning, Metis' was at the fence visiting her pony. Glenn called from the house to warn us that an unpredictable moose was in the yard with a hurt shoulder and he didn't know what it would do.

I went out the garage door to look around for Metis'. Here she came at a dead run, just a purple streak in her jacket. The moose was right behind her, trying to strike her with his front feet!

Mr. T. took off like a small black and white bullet. He started chewing on the moose's back hocks. The moose couldn't see his tormentor, but Mr. T ran him out into the woods. That moose never knew what had had him.

Mr. T wasn't very big, but there wasn't any other dogs his size that could compete with him as a loving, protector. Fiddlestix and Mr. T. are both gone now, but our entire family cherish memories of them.

Chapter 49

Russell's youngest daughter, Shaye, and her son, Shawn, had been to visit us in Anchorage several times, from their home in South Dakota. In the summer of 1982, Shawn came by himself when he was six. He and Metis' had a great time playing together. We bought Shawn a bicycle so that he could join Metis' on her rides to the back seventy acres of our place.

Metis' had found a tree that she called "the magic spruce". The tree was huge, with protective branches and a spot underneath, which was just right for the children to set up a little camp.

Metis' had a little broom and kept the dirt floor swept clean. They made tables and chairs from rocks. It didn't take them long to furnish their camp with pots and pans, rugs, dishes and some old blankets.

I had a horn, which I blew when I wanted them to check in. They knew that if I blew that horn, to hop onto their bikes and come back to the house. As soon as I was satisfied that they were O.K., they would pedal back to their camp in the forest, as fast as they could go.

They had made a pretend campfire out of wadded up red cellophane. With a Grandma like me, they knew better than to play with matches! I never had a problem with them trying, either.

That summer, the two of them went to Bible School. Shawn wasn't supposed to have sugar because his Mom thought it made him hyperactive. But, when they had their program and party at Bible School, Shawn had his plate overflowing with all the sweet goodies that everyone else had. He ate it all and was just fine.

Russell's mother, Vera, had come up the day before the Bible School program to spend three months with us. Our two mothers got along beautifully. We all had great visits and lots of fun.

Vera liked to stay home. She would often get into a baking mode as soon as everyone else left. Boy, did we have lots of goodies while she was at our house! Vera often made her special dessert, that she called "Cougan" for Russ I tried to make it once, but he said it wasn't nearly as good as his mother's. You'd better believe that I never tried to make it again, after that! (Cougan is custard with a bread dough crust and dried fruit filling).

Chapter 50

One beautiful winter afternoon, in 1987, Metis' and her friend were spending the weekend at our place. They had played school that morning, but wanted to go snowmachining after lunch.

So, I poured the last of the gas into my snowmachine, hooked up the sled, put in the old couch cushion for a pad, and took off. The girls took turns riding on the back, pretending that they were dog mushers. Every so often we stopped and had some of the hot cocoa and snacks we had brought with us. While we enjoyed this nourishment, we watched the moose below our hilltop. They were browsing on the birch and alder branches, as far up as they could stretch their necks.

In the background, the tops of the mountains, all around us, were glowing with different colors in the winter sun. God's hand was painting their snow-covered peaks. The setting was spectacular, but we had to get home before dark, so we ended our snowmachine trip. It was only about 5:00 p.m., but getting pretty dark. I parked the snowmachine and unloaded our now-empty containers. The roads were icy, and we still had to go the 15 miles to Wasilla for groceries. I decided to take our big Ford Bronco because it had four wheel drive. We were gone quite a while because we had stopped for dinner, too. When we got home and had put the groceries away, we were going to play a game, take a hot bubble bath and have Metis' and Michelle in bed by 9:00 p.m.

Glenn, Suzie and Brittany still lived in the old homestead house, but Glenn was gone, working on the North Slope. Soon, Suzie called and said that some dog musher wanted to use my snowmachine to run down his dog team, which had gotten away from him.

He had gotten knocked off, or fell off, the sled, and the fourteen or sixteen dogs had kept going. They had gotten tangled up in their harness and one had died. He got them back under control, then, they got away again. He had run all the way from the river, about two miles, with his warm gear and his bunny boots, which are real heavy and bulky.

He came to my door and rang the bell. When I opened the door, Mr. T (heavy on the "Mister") hit him in the chest! He asked if he could use my snowmachine to try to catch his dogs, because he was afraid they would go to the river and then he would never catch them. He was afraid that they would get tangled up in their harness, fight, or be so lost that they would starve to death.

I had ridden on the dogsled of my old friend and neighbor, Dick Smith, when he only had seven dogs pulling him, and I know they have unbelievable power. Dick's dogs were just a hobby, not racing dogs.

I told the man that I didn't have any more gas to put in the snowmachine, but we could take the Bronco, which was still warm. So, we got the girls loaded in the Bronco with us, and off we went. I asked him where he thought they were, and he was sure they had headed toward the river.

We had a trail going down the pole line, and it was pretty packed down from the snowmachines, so off we went down that pole line at about 45 miles per hour, over hill and dale. He kept urging me to go faster, until I told him that if we popped over one of the hills onto his team, we would run right over them.

He was very upset. He didn't speak English very well and it was hard for me to understand him, but I got the message that he was scared he would lose his team. If they got tangled, or fell through the ice, they would fight and he would lose them even if they stopped.

We were getting close to the river and the trail was gone. We were crashing through the alders. We thought all was lost. Just then, he spotted them! I asked him what I should do, and he said, "don't slow down, just keep driving right up beside them." So I did, against my better judgment. He fell out of the Bronco door right in the middle of his team. Somehow, he got on the sled they were still dragging and disappeared into the darkness.

Now, I had to wonder if I would end up stuck out there in the middle of nowhere with two little girls. But, again, God took care of us, and I was able to back up and with lots of careful maneuvering, got turned around and headed back home.

Soon the phone rang. It was Dick Smith, who told me that Martin Buser and his dogs had just stopped at his place and Martin was really dehydrated. Dick was giving him hot tea and orange juice, then would put Martin's dogs in the dog box on his pickup and take Martin, and his dogs, home.

That was the first time I knew that I had rescued Martin Buser, who had already run the Iditarod several times and has since been the champion three times. He told me later that some of those dogs we saved had been to Nome with him, and he had been on a training run to decide which should go again. I like to think that I had a part in his championships by helping his save his team that time!

Chapter 51

One summer, our friend Coker invited us to Homer to go halibut fishing on his boat. So, Glenn and Suzie and Rick and Paige planned to drive down together. But, I waited for Russ to get in from the North Slope, and then we flew down. The kids picked us up at the airport and all had dinner together. We went to our separate rooms to get some sleep and to get ready to meet Coker the next morning at 6:00 a.m.

It looked stormy, but there was very little wind. So, after a hearty breakfast, we headed for the docks. Homer has a big boat dock and it can be quite a job to load supplies if you have to make several trips. But, with our crew, we managed to get things loaded in one trip. After some hustling and bustling, we slowly cruised out of the harbor, down the canal and out to the open ocean.

We went out about three miles before Coker stopped and dropped anchor. After some confusion in getting set up, we set ourselves to catch the big one. Rick and I were at the front of the boat (I think they call it the "hull").

When I got a bite and tried to reel my line in, I couldn't budge it! I told Rick that my line must have snagged on a rock or something. He took my line, and after using a lot of muscle, he had my line coming up. There was a giant fish on the line! Rick was able to get it to the top of the water, and then the humongous fish just spit my hook out of its mouth and started to swim away.

I was yelling for a pitchfork or a gaffe, or something to hold onto this fish! They all yelled back that the only way to keep one that big was to shoot it in the head.

Everyone was excited and catching fish, and we never really noticed how rough the water was getting. Soon, Paige was sick. Then Suzie was sick. By that time, we brought all the poles on board and headed back to the safety of the harbor The waves were so big that we truly did feel like we were riding a cork in that endless ocean.

Then, to top it off really well, one of the engines on the boat quit! Coker was busy keeping the boat headed straight into the waves so that we wouldn't be swamped. Russell, Glenn and Rick got the tools out and the motor cover off and set about trying to get the dead motor going again.

The men never did get the motor started, but God and His angels got us back to the harbor at Homer safely.

I haven't been halibut fishing since, but I sure do like to eat it when friends give it to me!

Chapter 52

I was working at the local election at Houston City Hall, about 1985, and an older man, Dick Baggett, came in to vote. We got to talking and I found out that the local senior citizens center, Mid-Valley Senior Center, needed a cook to fill in while their cook was on vacation. He asked me if I would fill in for them, and, since I was ready to go back to work part time, I agreed.

At that time, they were having meals just three times per week, so I still had lots of time to enjoy my home.

The following spring, I took over as their cook and have been there ever since. I recently arranged to work two weeks on and two weeks off, so that I can help take care of Rick's children while he works on the North Slope and his wife, Paige, works in Palmer.

I have come to really love the folks and the senior center, and I know that they like me, too. (In fact, they told me that when I can't even leave when I die--they plan to have me "stuffed" and stand me by the stove in my usual position so that no one will know that I'm not really there!)

Mom had moved in with us after Dad had died, and had been with us for about ten years. Everyone was happy. Mom was so tiny that I could move her anywhere by myself.

She was suffering from heart failure. The last month of her life, Mr. T, and I slept with her.

One cold night, she told me to lift the covers so that Mr. T. could get under the covers and stay warm. I was afraid that he would accidentally scratch her, but she insisted. From then on, the dog slept under the covers with us.

Mom enjoyed being close to her grandchildren. She loved Glenn, Cindy and Rick so much. Cindy and her family had moved into the other side of the duplex. That meant that Mom also had her great-grandchildren close by, too. Metis' was about eight. Cindy's youngest, Chelsey, was just a baby and Glenn's oldest, Brittany, was a year old. Mom had plenty of children to love and keep her smiling.

Then, one Saturday morning before Thanksgiving, I was to prepare the annual community dinner at the senior center.

Mom wasn't very well and couldn't eat her toast or drink her orange juice.

I told her that I would just run down (about three miles) to the Center to put the turkey in the oven and make the stuffing, then would be right back.

I knew that she would be looked after, as both Russell and Cindy were there. I no more than had gotten to the senior center than Russell came and told me that Mom had died. He had carried her to the couch and he had thought she was asleep. Then, Cindy came over to check on her, and after a few seconds they saw that she wasn't breathing. She looked so peaceful. Her soul had slipped away to heaven to be with God and my Dad and her other relatives who had gone before her to be with God.

There was a big void in the house without that beloved, sweet, beautiful, little lady in our lives. She had passed away the day before she was 74.

Chuck was stuck in Chicago in a blizzard and couldn't join me in Alaska to help take Mom back to South Dakota to be buried.. I told him to just meet me in Spearfish as I would take her back there to be buried beside my Dad and the rest of her family. I did, and was back to work in just a couple of weeks.

Chapter 53

On a crisp, cold morning on the Alaskan homestead that we were living on, I had gotten my warm clothes on and was tending to my pet goats, our old, chubby, Chinese pug, ZeeZee, and our beautiful white Spitz, King, that we had rescued from abandonment.

King went into a fit of barking in the high pitch, which is unique to his breed. Suddenly, I heard the door bell ring, and when I went to answer it, I saw outside a young woman whose face was covered with a blue scarf. Tears were flowing from her eyes and she was so distraught that I thought she had been in a car accident on the nearby busy highway. We often get people in trouble at our door, and I always try to help them, if I can. So, I invited her in.

When she got inside, she asked, in a quivering voice if I was Phyllis Dilley. I assured her that I was the person she was looking for. By then, she was sobbing so hard that I had to help her into my kitchen. I took her coat and got her some coffee.

After a few minutes, she was able to whisper; " I need your help. I can't live like this. I can't go on." By this time, she had removed the scarf and I could immediately see what her problem was. I recognized the new skin graft scars on her face as being similar to the ones I had had. Her upper lip was pulled to the right side in a grotesque manner. Knowing that she would not be able to drink from a cup, I got a straw for her coffee.

I took my own coffee and sat down at the table with her. All the memories of that time over twenty years ago came flooding back--all the horror, pain and complete hopelessness of a situation over which you have absolutely no control. That time had really been the end of my life, as I had known it. I remembered that I had told the doctors that I would be willing to help others who were going through the trauma of having been burned, and the aftermath of scars and acceptance. Now, I had an opportunity to do that.

The young lady told me that her name was Sarah Adams (name changed to protect her privacy) and that all that could be done for her had been done. She went on to tell me that the doctor at the hospital told her to call me, but she didn't know what to say, or how I could help her. In spite of that, she found out where I lived. It took her quite a period of time before she had the courage to make the drive to our home because she didn't know how I would react to being reminded of my own horrible time.

Soon, she started telling her story.
Sarah and her girlfriend, Jean (name changed to protect her privacy) had rented a camper for the weekend. They had camped beside the beautiful rushing creek at Hatcher Pass.

It was a chilly, damp day, so they decided to start the furnace so the camper would be warm when they came back from their hike. They enjoyed their hike, and after a couple of hours, went back to the camper. As soon as Sarah reached up and opened the camper door, she heard a loud

BOOM! A fireball hit the right side of her face. Jean wasn't injured and hurried to another campsite for someone to rush them to the hospital. It turned out that Sarah had third degree burns (the worst kind) on four square inches of her cheek and lip.

She had gone through the ordeal of treatment and skin grafts. After the skin grafts had shrunk, her lower eyelid was pulled down and her upper lip was pulled up. To me, she just looked like she had had a bad burn, but to Sarah, her life was completely destroyed. She didn't yet accept the fact that with time, the scars would heal and fade and that they could be stretched with massage and petroleum jelly.

She had worked as a paralegal in a downtown law office and had enjoyed an active social life as a beautiful woman. Now, she didn't plan on working again, for fear of how her appearance would affect the clients, or her co-workers, at the firm where she had worked. She felt ugly and was sure everyone else would consider her to be ugly.

By now, she was crying again, and begged me to tell her my story. She told me that my scars didn't look so bad and that I seemed to be happy and busy. She asked me if I wasn't afraid of what people say about the way I look.

I began by telling Sarah that the whole secret of her healing lies deep within. I told her that beauty really is only skin deep. It takes a while to realize that when you've been attractive and proud all your life. I knew, because I had been there.

I went on to tell her that the scars would fade in time and that the best thing she could do was just get back to living her everyday life. I explained that the people close to her wouldn't even notice her scars and strangers would just wonder how she got burned. I assured her that her injury would always be obvious to have been from burns.

I told Sarah about my fantastic life with Dave and about our three wonderful children. I shared memories with her about our happiness and the fun we had had as a family--the horseback rides, the snowmachining, the fishing, and all the other family-oriented activities we all did together. We had lived comfortably, even though we didn't have a lot of money. What we had lacked in money was more than made up in love.

I told Sarah about the family tradition of Dave, our boys and his closest friends all going moose hunting together the end of each August, when the season opened.

I went on to tell her about the hunt which proved to be fatal to Dave and which changed me forever.

So, I finished my time with Sarah by telling her that her scars would heal. I told her to get on with her life and not to sweat the small things. Some people who were burned came to visit me in the hospital, and whenever the doctors asked me to, I went to visit other patients, too. I learned that my doctor used my case to become certified in working with burn patients. It gives hope to keep going on when we encourage each other.

I told Sarah that beauty really is only skin deep, and asked her to let her real beauty shine through from within.

When I finished my story and advice to Sarah, I took out my picture albums and showed her my real treasures --my three children and seven grandchildren. They are treasures from God and couldn't care less what I look like on the outside, they know that I love them from the inside.

I often think of Sarah and I hope that everyone who reads my story and who is hurting from disfigurement, or any other ailment can know that God is with them, and his angels will see them through, just like they did me.

EPILOGUE

For those who wonder how we came to live on the homestead property, and what our family is doing and where they're living, I'll bring you up to date.

The forty acres adjoining the front of our seventy acres had come up for sale. It was another part of Rose Palmquist's original homestead and still had her homestead house on it.

We enjoyed going to the property from Anchorage whenever we could, and stayed in the old house. It wasn't long before Glenn moved into the house and Rick moved his mobile home onto the property, close by.

When Glenn and Suzie got married, in 1975, they lived in the old house. And in a couple of years had their first little girl, Brittany. Now, I really knew why God had let me live! I had two beautiful blessings in my granddaughters.

Brittany was a "Lady Godiva" type, who couldn't stand to wear clothes, but she had no hair to cover herself with. As soon as she was big enough, she took all her clothes off, every chance she got. She left a trail of clothes from the homestead house to ours. Her little black puppy sat patiently while she removed each piece of clothing.

Mark Riley had been a friend of Glenn and Rick's for years. One day he called and wanted to talk to Cindy, instead of the boys. I was shocked. I even asked him why he wanted to talk to Cindy!

As time went on, they got married and I approved fully. Mark adopted Metis' and has treated her so wonderfully. He is a good, hardworking man who is so different than the other fellow was. The next year, they had a little girl they named Chelsey. She and Brittany are just a year apart. Another of God's blessings in the form of a granddaughter had come my way!

The boys started a company, which did dirt work, and built a big shop to work on their equipment. They did very well until they subcontracted a major job near Anchorage with a company from Seattle. It turned out that the company from Seattle got their money, but never paid the sub-contractors. The boys lost everything and it took them a long time to get over that loss and move on.

At that time, there wasn't a law in Alaska, which required proof that the subcontractors had been paid before the contractor got their final check. I hope there is now.

Russ and I decided to build a simple duplex on five acres on the front of the forty acres for us. We made it a point not to have any stairs for Mom to worry about climbing in her condition. We built the garage in the middle of the two units, so it's very private for the renters, as well as ourselves.

Russ was still working on the North Slope at that time, and rotated his shift every week, or two, depending on what his work called for. He is now retired from working on the North

Slope, but every summer he hauls dirt for Fisher's Fuel and the Dirt Company, just down the road from us.

Mark and Cindy bought our house in Anchorage. But they later sold it so that they could build on Big Beaver Lake. While they made that house livable, they lived in our apartment. Mark works on the North Slope and they now live with Chelsey at Big Beaver Lake. It's less than a mile through the trails from our place to theirs, but it's about eleven miles by maintained road. Metis' is a hair stylist and lives in Anchorage. She loves to travel and has been all over the world and throughout the United States

When Russ and I go to South Dakota, we stay at his daughter Tammy's home. Shaye is now a nurse and Tammy a schoolteacher in Rapid City, South Dakota. They both have good husbands and we really love the grandkids that are in South Dakota.

Tammy's girls play the violin in the winter, but their summers are filled with softball. In 1998, their team won the State championship in South Dakota!

The family grew some more when Glenn and Suzie had Caalee. She was such a tiny thing! She inherited my love for all kinds of critters.

Rick married his old school girlfriend, Paige. In a couple of years, they had a little girl that they named Aryel. She has the most beautiful green eyes and real dark, thick hair like Rick's. She is the paperwork lover of the family--always playing "office" or "school".

Then, Glenn and Suzie had a third little girl (and I do mean little girl!), who is such a delight. She is full of mischief and energy and is so loving.

We were happy with all our granddaughters, and then Rick and Paige gave us our grandson, David. We worried some that with all the girl cousins who liked to play house and "dress-up" that David would be in danger of being their model, but we shouldn't have worried, he was all boy from the minute he was born! He loves construction equipment of any kind.

David has asthma, but with proper treatment, it doesn't slow him down much. He likes to ride on and "drive" heavy equipment with his Dad. He also entered, and won, the world's longest "kitty-cat" snowmachine race. He won the competition for the four to six age group when he was four.

One day, when he was three, he came running through the house pretending that he was "riding" a potato chip between his legs pretending that it was a stick-horse! I decided that I could do better than that, so hand made a stick horse with a real-looking head, for him. Of course, I had to make one for each of the grandchildren. It is really hard for me to use a needle, but I love to make those stick horses for the children. In fact, I had so much demand for them that I made and sold some, and gave a lot away to friends. I call the handmade stick horses "Fiddlestix" in memory of Metis' pony.

David and Laurel are the champion stick horse riders in the group of cousins. They ride them so much, and so hard, that I have to replace the sticks in their mounts pretty often.

Rick, Paige and the children live in the subdivision we put in on the back of our property.

Glenn and Suzie with their girls, Brittany, Caalee and Laurel, live on the Willow side of the Hatcher Pass Road and operate a coffee shop there. Because that is a popular area for snowmachining and other winter sports, they cater to them, as well as the tourists who drive over the pass during the summer. Glenn still does other jobs, like road building, to supplement their income. They don't have electricity, so he has to be home every night to tend to their generator

The cousins all like to have slumber parties at my house. We often take bike rides or go snowmachining together, depending upon the season. I've even been known to join the stickhorse riding group once in awhile. Sometimes my kitchen table turns into a worktable for budding artists, or camping tents are constructed from blankets and chairs in the middle of our not-very-big living room. I try to teach some of my favorite songs to the grandchildren, but since the crash, I can no longer play the guitar. My voice used to really be good, but a squawk is more my style now, with the scars in my throat and vocal cords.

Boy, do I ever enjoy the country life! I get to mow a lawn, which gets bigger each year (and I look back while I mow!), sometimes I have goats or other critters. Russell feeds lots of birds each winter and we enjoy having a place for the grandchildren to run and explore and use their imaginations while they play outside. In fact, the grandchildren enjoy our place so much that they don't like to leave--just like I enjoyed being at my grandparents' homes.

Our whole family went to South Dakota for a family reunion a few years ago. My children's spouses and children had never been there before. They loved the beauty of the Black Hills where I grew up. It was wonderful having the whole family together, and showing them where I came from.

My brother, his lovely wife Franny, and their three boys live in Massachusetts.
We meet once a year in South Dakota so that we can see each other and the remaining family and friends that live there.

Betty and Loren, Dave's sister and brother-in-law still live in Anchorage and we get together as often as possible.

As I write this I am still working two weeks on and two weeks off, at Mid-Valley Senior Center, in Houston, Alaska, which now serves meals five evenings each week, and has a beautiful big building and is building housing for low-income senior citizens,.

The senior center is such a homey place. I love each and every one of the senior citizens and staff. All the employees there work really hard to make it a place with an atmosphere of love and caring. We have a lot of fun and the senior citizens get a good, tasty, balanced supper. God bless them, one and all.

Helen Bowles is the cook who alternates with me while I look after Aryel and David. I make sure that David gets his asthma treatments on a real regular schedule. Helen also takes care of her grandchildren on her two weeks off. It works out really well for both of our families and us.

The Project Director at the senior center, Elsie O'Bryan, is also a dear friend of mine. She has helped throughout this book writing process. Without her, this story would never have gotten onto paper, because I can't type anymore, or run a computer. I wrote the story out in long hand and she filled in the gaps--thank goodness we have worked together for lots of years and she is used to my handwriting and interpreting what I really mean! She is very familiar with my family and has heard these stories many times around our dining room table, which made it easier for her to help me pull it all together.

When she published her own book of poetry, she put together "Bear Paw Publishing" and is the publisher of my story. Thanks, Elsie, for all your expertise and caring.

I started writing this story down in 1996, but was interrupted by the Miller's Reach wildfire, which burned many trees on our property, as well as three homes in our subdivision (including Rick's partially finished house, which they weren't living in yet). Over four hundred homes in all burned before the fire was controlled nearly a week after it started. The park-like setting is now destroyed, but God is putting things back in place to be beautiful again. With our labor and love, it will be restored. There are things, which will never be replaced though, like some of Dave's old implements that I cherished.

Dave's old mechanical "farm hand" had been hanging between two beautiful birch trees on the back part of the homestead near where we had usually planted oats. That had been my spot where I had gone by myself each Memorial Day to pray and to leave one yellow rose for my lost love. But, it burned during the Miller's Reach Wildfire.

I now take Dave's rose to the old dump rake that is near the house. I use the old implement to honor the many fun family times we spent working with those common implements that have become treasures to me.

God has seen to it that the dump rake won't be moved, because a new birch tree is growing through a hole in the old seat.

I said my final good-bye to Dave years ago, but I still have feelings of sadness and I will always remember our life and love together.

But, we all have to get on with our lives, no matter what trials we face. God wants us to be strong, and to do His will.

All in all, when I think about what I've been through and about my family, friends, home and work, I'm content with what God has brought my way.

Suzie and Glenn Dilley; Caalee, Brittany and Laurel Dilley

Mark and Cindy Riley; Metis' and Chelsey Riley and Ripper

Rick and Paige Dilley; Aryel and David Dilley

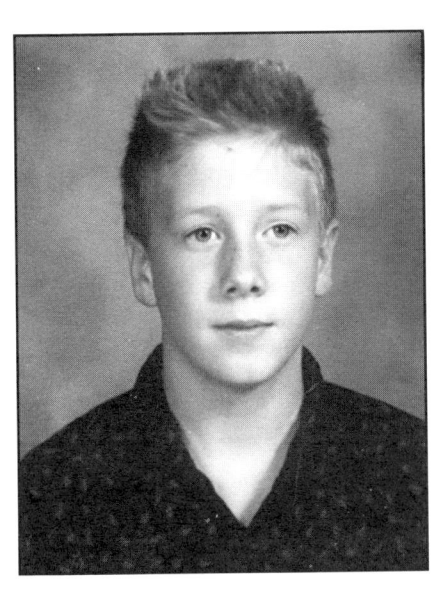

Shaun Mathis, Shaye's son;
Courtney and Cassidy Klein, Tammy's Daughters
Loren and Betty Dodds, Dave Dilley's brother-in-law and sister

Aryel Dilley playing in the snow with Amos and Andy (goats) and ZeeZee (dog)

ABOUT THE AUTHOR

Phyllis Barker Dilley Backhaus, 62 at the time of the writing of this book has drawn from a lifetime of memories, both good and bad, in the telling of these tales.

Her three children, now grown, provided the incentive and determination (along with her being purely stubborn) for her refusal to submit to the effects of severe burns and the death of their father in tragic circumstances.

She has taken her scars and turned them into badges of inspiration for her many friends and associates.

Rick Dilley, Cindy Riley, Phyllis Backhaus & Glenn Dilley